THE WRITER'S NOTEBOOK II

Craft Essays
from
Tin House

THE

WRITER'S NOTEBOOK II

Tin House Books

Published by Tin House Books, Portland, Oregon,
and New York, New York
Distributed to the trade by Publishers Group West,
1700 Fourth St., Berkeley, CA 94710,
www.pgw.com

First U.S. edition 2012
Interior design by Elyse Strongin, Neuwirth & Associates, Inc.
Printed in the USA

www.tinhouse.com

CONTENTS

Introduction | FRANCINE PROSE   1

Beginnings | ANN HOOD   5

Don't Write What
You Know | BRET ANTHONY JOHNSTON   19

Funny Is the New Deep:
An Exploration of the Comic Impulse | STEVE ALMOND   31

Research in Fiction | ANDREA BARRETT   43

The Sword of Damocles: On Suspense, Shower Murders,
and Shooting People on the Beach | ANTHONY DOERR   57

"A Sort of Leaning Against":
Writing With, From, and For Others | MAGGIE NELSON   83

The Experience In Between:
Thoughts on Nonlinear Narrative | ADAM BRAVER   105

On the Making of Orchards | AIMEE BENDER   115

Get a Job: The Importance of Work in Prose and Poetry | BENJAMIN PERCY   131

Short Story: A Process of Revision | ANTONYA NELSON   141

There Interposed a _____: A Few Considerations of Poetic Drama | MARY SZYBIST   157

Story & Dream | JIM KRUSOE   173

Do Something | CHRISTOPHER R. BEHA   187

Engineering Impossible Architectures | KAREN RUSSELL   197

Endings: Parting Is Such Sweet Sorrow | ELISSA SCHAPPELL   217

Contributors   237

Copyright Notes and Permissions   243

THE WRITER'S NOTEBOOK II

INTRODUCTION

FRANCINE PROSE

WHY SHOULD IT seem surprising that if we want to know what writers think—really think—about writing, we should read more of what they write and listen less to what they say? Having been a speaker, an audience member, an interviewer and an interviewee at the question-and-answer sessions that so often follow literary readings and panels, I have witnessed, and been responsible for, those moments when a writer takes the easy way out and simply repeats a facile statement she's made before, or blurts out something to fill the silence, whether or not it's true.

Writers are creatures who (to paraphrase Wordsworth) function best when we can recall the writing process in tranquility. Which isn't to say that the experience of sitting in front of the blank page or screen is necessarily a tranquil one, unless you are the sort of masochist who finds peace in hideous anguish. Still, the closest writers may ever come to saying something accurate, let alone useful, about what we do is when we are alone, at our desks, in private—when we write the sort of essays collected in *The Writer's Notebook II.*

I think it's probably safe to say that most writers would rather lose themselves in a story or a poem than remain in the prison of their conscious selves and attempt to describe what we do. And though most writers would rather write a story or a poem than an essay about writing a story or a poem, the fact is that we are occasionally—thanks to teaching or lecture commitments, a deadline or an invitation—moved to think about this bizarre activity that is at once our life's blood and our job.

Nor should it come as a great surprise that writers can actually write, even when they are writing about writing. Each of the essays in this collection finds its unique voice in the way that each author chooses to place one word after another—vocabulary and punctuation decisions, matters of tone and diction, of perspective, detail, and length. The way in which these essays are written are lessons in themselves, lessons that reach us, above and beyond the substance of what their authors are saying.

You can open *The Writer's Notebook II* at random and find some sentence that will surprise or delight you, a phrase or paragraph that will make you think, or laugh out loud. Or both. Here is Elissa Schappell on what may be the all-time worst ending in the history of fiction: "There is a tale, now legendary in the circles of teachers of creative writing, about a story that ends with the revelation that the story was being narrated by a squirrel with a bag on its head." And Steve Almond on a young writer's desire to be taken seriously: "If enough people took me seriously I might start to take myself seriously, thereby dispelling the notion, forever lurking at the gates of ambition, that I was a sad clown who should quit writing and return to my given career as a professional masturbator, a career for which I am even now somewhat nostalgic." And listen to Karen Russell on the richness with which literature excites and satisfies a child's imagination: "As a kid growing up in Miami, I lived in the closet of my mind, trying on costumes . . . I wanted scales and wings. I'd figured out that you could do these really bizarre tricks in the library, in full view of the imperturbably cheerful librarians. You could, for example, metamorphose. You could suture a character's wings to your eight-year-old body. You could drop time like a skirt and step outside its wrinkled orbit."

If one had to find a common thread stitched through all, or most, of these intensely individual essays, it might wind its way around the question of how much writers read—and how much inspiration they take from the work of their predecessors. Maggie Nelson pays tribute to the poetry of Alice Notley and Anne Carson; Mary Szybist contributes thoughtful and perceptive readings of Emily Dickinson and John Ashbery; Jim Krusoe views an array of literary masterpieces through the lens of the dream; Bret Anthony Johnston examines the magic with which Tim O'Brien and Lorrie Moore alchemize experience into art; Ann Hood takes us on a lively tour of introductory sentences, from the familiar beginnings of *Anna Karenina* and *Pride and Prejudice* to the less often quoted but no less arresting introductions to *Mrs. Dalloway* and *Elmer Gantry*. Anthony Doerr looks to Camus's novel *The Stranger* and to Joyce Carol Oates's story "Where Are You Going, Where Have You Been?" for instruction—which he kindly passes on to us—in how to build and maintain suspense. And Christopher R. Beha transcribes an extraordinarily beautiful and useful passage from Saint Augustine about, as Beha puts it, "the beauty to be found in a well-made whole."

Much of what any writer needs to know is contained in this helpful book. Andrea Barrett muses on the pleasures of research, the challenges and rewards of incorporating history into one's work. Benjamin Percy considers the importance of work itself—the jobs that people do: "Writing is an act of empathy. You are occupying and understanding a point of view that might be alien to your own—and work is often the keyhole through which you peer." Adam Braver describes the experience of editing a manuscript with the aid of a pair of scissors and a roll of Scotch tape. Antonya Nelson comes as close as anyone ever has to describing how she—or anyone—writes as she tells us about a class in which she asked her students to "undertake the process of writing that I myself undertake."

In her essay "On the Making of Orchards," Aimee Bender quotes a line from Dante suggesting that art is God's grandchild. After finishing the last of these essays, we may all feel a little closer to being the distant relatives of art or nature or God. Reading *The Writer's Notebook II* is like spending a couple of hours or days or weeks in the company of writers whose voices you want in your head, whose words you want to keep beside your desk. Go ahead, they seem to be saying. Here is how writing has been for me, and this is what I've learned. Consider this, think about that, read the books that have inspired me. I'm going to tell you what I know, but the rest is up to you. All you have to do now is just sit down—and begin.

BEGINNINGS

ANN HOOD

I CANNOT WRITE an essay, a short story, or even a novel until I know my first line. At night, I put myself to sleep rearranging words, inserting a comma and then taking it out again. I edit and revise that one sentence while I cook dinner, wait in the car for my kids to walk out of school, do the laundry. The pressure of getting that sentence right is enormous. In fact, not just that sentence, but the opening paragraph—no, the opening page—has to do so much that in some ways it is the most important thing to write.

The beginning introduces the protagonist and his or her conflict. It creates tone, point of view, setting, voice. It introduces themes. Or, as Ted Kooser explains in *The Poetry Home Repair Manual*, the opening is the hand you extend to your reader. When the writer John Irving told me that he always knew his first line before he began writing, because by knowing his first line he then knew his last line, I understood yet another burden of the beginning: it puts into motion the events that will drive the story to its resolution. And that resolution is often the inverse of the opening.

No wonder I spend so much time on getting the beginning right.

Yet, after I've finished a story and started the revision process, I almost always find myself right back at the beginning, reworking it again. While I was writing, characters changed, new ideas intruded, mistakes in the original plan revealed themselves, and sometimes a different story altogether has taken over. In his book *The Triggering Town*, the poet Richard Hugo says that there are actually two beginnings: the one that comes from your initiating or triggering subject and the one that is generated as you write and discover your real subject. Your challenge is to let go of your triggering beginning and find your real one. This is why in writing workshops a common comment is "Your story actually begins on page five (or three or ten)."

Once I've found my true subject, I have to redetermine the best way to begin. That perfect sentence I spent so much time crafting isn't necessarily gone; sometimes it appears later in the scene or the chapter, or becomes the beginning of chapter two. Kooser warns about those "perfect" openings. We polish them so much, he says, that they become the best part, with everything else weak in comparison. It is almost a relief to let it go and turn my attention to all the different options for how to begin now that I know where I'm headed.

Probably the best way to consider these options is to go to your bookshelf and open your favorite books to see how they start. What is the opening line? What literary device does the writer use to get started? How does the opening line lead into the ones that follow? What is the overall effect of the beginning? For the purpose of illustrating the options for beginnings,

I did just that. I went to my bookshelf and read beginnings, considering these questions as I mentally categorized them. As evidence to the effect of a good beginning, I began this exercise when the sun was shining so brightly that I had to adjust the blinds. The next time I looked up, it was late afternoon and the sun had dipped in the sky. Hours lost in the promise those beginnings set forth.

The options I've landed on fall into these categories: Introduction, An Old Saw, Character Description, A Setting, In Media Res, Facts, A Truism or Philosophical Idea, Dialogue, Overture, and Otherworld. You will see as you read examples of each of these that, in fact, they overlap. For example, the first line of J. D. Salinger's *The Catcher in the Rye* could easily fit into three or four. So the point isn't to pigeonhole beginnings, or to set rules for what constitutes the ones I've chosen here. Rather, these examples will hopefully get you thinking about how you can begin your stories. They are meant to inspire and clarify, not to serve as strict definitions.

Introduction

"Call me Ishmael."

"I am an invisible man."

"You don't know about me without you have read a book by the name of The Adventures of Tom Sawyer; but that ain't no matter."

"If you really want to hear about it, the first thing you'll probably want to know is where I was born, and what my lousy childhood was like, and how my parents were occupied and all before they had me, and all that David Copperfield kind of crap, but I don't feel like going into it, if you want to know the truth."

Herman Melville in *Moby-Dick*, Ralph Ellison in *Invisible Man*, Mark Twain in *The Adventures of Huckleberry Finn*, and Salinger in *The Catcher in the Rye* all begin their novels with the protagonist introducing himself. And the way in which Ishmael, Ellison's nameless protagonist, Huck, and Holden introduce themselves sets the tone for the rest of the novel. It also creates a storytelling voice that reveals character. Ishmael's order, Huck's socioeconomic class and education, Holden's sassiness are immediately apparent from the first line. In this type of beginning, it is even possible to reveal the work's themes, as Richard Ford does in *The Sportswriter*. The opening lines, "My name is Frank Bascombe. I am a sportswriter," are followed by what on the surface appears to be unimportant information: Frank Bascombe tells us his address and how long he's lived there, that he bought the house with money he received when his book was made into a movie, that he and his wife and children are set up to live "the good life." But these seemingly minor details tell the reader everything that Bascombe values—being a man, his work, his home and sense of place, his relationship with his family, and his expectation of "the good life." By using an introduction as the beginning, Ford intimates that these very values will be challenged in the novel.

An Old Saw

THINK OF CLASSIC opening lines and "Once upon a time . . ." almost immediately comes to mind. Fans of the *Peanuts* comic strip may also remember Snoopy beginning his novel again and again, always starting with the line "It was a dark and stormy night." Our instincts may warn us to stay away from such cliché beginnings, and for the most part those instincts are correct. In fact, since 1982, San Jose State University has run a writing contest inspired by "It was a dark and stormy night." The contest, named for Sir Edward George Earle Lytton Bulwer-Lytton, who began his 1830 novel, *Paul Clifford*, with those lines, calls for the worst opening lines for the worst of all possible novels.

Yet Charles Dickens opens stave one of *A Christmas Carol* with "Once upon a time . . . old Scrooge sat busy in his counting house" to set the magical tone and actions of the story. Similarly, James Joyce's *A Portrait of the Artist As a Young Man* begins: "Once upon a time and a very good time it was there was a moocow coming down along the road and this moocow that was coming down along the road met a nicens little boy named baby tuckoo." Contemporary writers have also returned to these old saws as openings: the first line in Anne Tyler's *Back When We Were Grownups* is "Once upon a time, there was a woman who discovered she had turned into the wrong person," and Madeleine L'Engle begins *A Wrinkle in Time* with the very words "It was a dark and stormy night." By using what we might consider clichés, writers can immediately set the tone of the work, allude to those older stories, and make something fresh out of a time-worn beginning.

Character Description

WHEN A STORY opens with a character description, the writer is sending a signal to readers that this person is going to be important, forcing us to take notice. The writer wants us to pay attention to the character's actions, the way he or she looks or talks or thinks, as Chekhov does when he opens his short story "The Birthday Party" with a detailed description of Olga Mikhailovna's perspective of her husband's birthday party. These details—"The obligation to smile and talk continuously, the stupidity of the servants, the clatter of dishes, the long intervals between courses, and the corset she had put on to conceal her pregnancy from her guests"—delay the action of the story but give great insight into the character of Olga.

In her novel *Inventing the Abbots*, Sue Miller uses this description of Lloyd Abbot to introduce not only his character but also the novel's themes: "Lloyd Abbot wasn't the richest man in our town, but he had, in his daughters, a vehicle for displaying his wealth that some of the richer men didn't have."

Jane Gardam uses two different techniques of character description in her novel *Old Filth*. The book opens with a two-page scene, written in play form, in which characters discuss a man—Old Filth—who has just left the room. They reveal Old Filth's age ("He must be a hundred."), his former occupation ("Great advocate, judge and—bit of a wit."), and a description ("Magnificent looks, though. And still sharp."). Then Gardam moves on to a traditional chapter, which begins: "He was spectacularly clean. You might say ostentatiously clean." She continues with physical details—"His shoes shone like conkers," "He had the elegance of the 1920s," "Always yellow cotton or silk socks from Harrods"—

and then describes his personality, his career path, and finally his marriage. These opening pages give the reader both a description of Old Filth as he seems to others and a third-person omniscient view of him before the action begins. This not only creates a thorough character description, but it also makes the reader curious to read on and discover why Old Filth is so important.

Setting

I HAVE ALWAYS loved the way John Steinbeck opens *Of Mice and Men*: "A few miles south of Soledad, the Salinas River drops in close to the hillside bank and runs deep and green." Steinbeck continues to describe the setting until we see the clearing by the stream where animals come to rest or drink. Two men then enter the scene, and their stories are revealed. There is something cinematic in beginning this way, as if we are watching through a panoramic lens that slowly focuses on the characters in the setting.

The first line of Stephen Crane's *The Red Badge of Courage* has a similar effect: "The cold passed reluctantly from the earth, and the retiring fogs revealed an army stretched out on the hills, resting." As does Ernest Hemingway's opening line in *A Farewell to Arms*: "In the late summer of that year we lived in a house in a village that looked across the river and the plain to the mountains."

Opening with setting can also allow for the introduction of metaphors and themes used in the book to be presented immediately, as Edith Wharton does in *Ethan Frome*. The first chapter begins with the description of a cold, bleak New England landscape: "The village lay under two feet of snow, with drifts at the windy corners. In a sky of iron the points of the Dipper hung like icicles and Orion flashed his cold fires. The moon had set, but the night was so transparent that the white house-fronts between the elms looked gray against the snow, clumps of bushes made black stains on it, and the basement windows of the church sent shafts of yellow light far across the endless undulations." Into this setting walks young Ethan Frome. The novel's plot revolves around Frome's desire for a woman who is not his wife. At first, he appreciates the loveliness of winter. However, he eventually realizes that he is oppressed by the elements. These very themes and metaphors are suggested by the opening description of the setting. Wharton uses images of black and white, fire and ice, and the church to set up the moral and social conflicts Frome will face.

In Media Res

WRITING WORKSHOPS OFTEN advise students to employ Horace's missive to begin in medias res, in the middle of things. Often, this advice is given to keep beginning writers from opening with too much backstory. But for all writers, opening in medias res is a good way to get the story moving. This technique for beginnings is so popular that it is difficult to choose which examples to use to illustrate it.

Anthony Burgess's *Earthly Powers* opens with "It was the afternoon of my eighty-first birthday, and I was in bed with my catamite when Ali announced that the archbishop had come to see me." Burgess does not begin with the eighty years that came before. He does not begin with that morning. He begins at the moment the archbishop arrives, the moment when things are about to change. Hunter S. Thompson does something similar in the first line of *Fear and Loathing in Las Vegas*: "We were somewhere around Barstow on the edge of the desert when the drugs began to take hold." He doesn't begin with the characters preparing for a trip; he begins somewhere around Barstow, when the drugs take hold—the moment when things begin to change.

Arguably the most quoted first line in discussions of beginnings is the opening of Gabriel Garcia Marquez's *One Hundred Years of Solitude*: "Many years later, as he faced the firing squad, Colonel Aureliano Buendía was to remember that distant afternoon when his father took him to discover ice." The reason this line is so effective and memorable—in addition to the beautiful writing and the compelling setup—is that it manages to start the novel in medias res and to introduce backstory simultaneously. Buendia is facing the firing squad *and* remembering the distant afternoon when his father took him to discover ice.

Facts

To begin a piece by stating a fact might not sound very writerly, but, actually, this seemingly simple technique carries a great deal of weight. The fact that opens the work must be the most important detail of the story. It must inform the reader, reveal character or plot, suggest something large and vital. When Pat Conroy opens *The Lords of Discipline* with the fact "I wear the ring," he is—in just four words—revealing everything you need to know about the plot, which revolves around the activities at a military school in the South and the issues of loyalty and betrayal signified by the importance of that ring. He accomplishes a similar feat in *The Prince of Tides*, which opens with this fact: "My wound is geography." Those four words contain the theme of the novel, which is discovering what it means to be a southern man and how to live with that burden.

Consider the facts that open *Elmer Gantry* by Sinclair Lewis: "Elmer Gantry was drunk."; *Mrs. Dalloway* by Virginia Woolf: "Mrs. Dalloway said she would buy the flowers herself."; and *The Old Man and the Sea* by Ernest Hemingway: "He was an old man who fished alone in a skiff in the Gulf Stream and he had gone eighty-four days now without taking a fish." Brief and declarative, these facts reveal everything we need to know about the novel and its protagonist.

A Truism or Philosophical Idea

SIMILAR TO BEGINNING with a fact, stating a truism or philosophical idea is another way to open your story, such as the first line of *Anna Karenina* by Leo Tolstoy: "Happy families are all alike; every unhappy family is unhappy in its own way." Or *Pride and Prejudice* by Jane Austen: "It is a truth universally acknowledged, that a single man in possession of a good fortune must be in want of a wife." Or even *A Tale of Two Cities* by Charles Dickens, which begins, "It was the best of times, it was the worst of times, it was the age of wisdom, it was the age of foolishness, it was the epoch of belief, it was the epoch of incredulity, it was the season of Light, it was the season of Darkness, it was the spring of hope, it was the winter of despair."

Unlike beginning with a fact, when you begin with a truism or a philosophical idea you rely on generalities rather than specific details. The burden of such an opening is that the work must then prove the idea to be true. The theme is laid out at the start, and the promise the writer makes to the reader is that, by the story's end, it will be clear in what ways unhappy families are different from each other, that single wealthy men want wives, and why the times were so contradictory.

Dialogue

BEGINNING WITH DIALOGUE is one of the most difficult ways to open a story successfully. The dialogue must be compelling enough to draw the reader in before he or she knows anything about the character(s) speaking or the context in which the dialogue is taking place. There exists the danger that the dialogue will feel disembodied or separate from what follows.

Difficult, but not impossible, as Salman Rushdie demonstrates in *The Satanic Verses*, which opens with this line of dialogue: "'To be born again,' sang Gibreel Farishta tumbling from the heavens, 'first you have to die.'" And Katherine Dunn in *Geek Love*: "'When your mama was the geek, my dreamlets,' Papa would say, 'she made the nipping off of noggins such a crystal mystery that the hens themselves yearned toward her, waltzing around her, hypnotized with longing.'"

Why do these openings work? First, the speakers—Gibreel Farishta and Papa—are identified by name. In this way, the reader is introduced to the character who is speaking, which prevents that disembodied feeling. But perhaps even more importantly, *what* they are saying and *how* they say it draws the reader in immediately. With *The Satanic Verses*, we wonder if the speaker is dead. And we are given the wonderful added detail that Gibreel is tumbling from heaven. Papa's dialogue is strange and charming at the same time. Mama was a geek? The nipping off of noggins? Hens yearned toward her? Both of these beginnings make the reader want to find out what will happen next.

Overture

RON HANSEN DESCRIBES the type of beginning he uses in his novel *The Assassination of Jesse James by the Coward Robert Ford* as an "overture opening." Hansen begins by writing everything he knows about Jesse James, including that James walked around the house with several newspapers, stuffed flat pencils in his pockets, flipped peanuts to squirrels, braided dandelions into his wife's yellow hair, sucked raw eggs out of their shells, and ate grass when he was sick.

An overture-style opening is also used by John Hawkes in *Second Skin* when the narrator tells us all of the things he loves: "the hummingbird that darts to the flower beyond the rotted sill where my feet are propped; lover of bright needlepoint and the bright stitching fingers of humorless old ladies bent to their sweet and infamous designs; lover of parasols made from the same puffy stuff as a young girl's underdrawers; still lover of that small naval boat which somehow survived the distressing years of my life between her decks or in her pilothouse; and also lover of poor dear black Sonny, my mess boy, fellow victim and confidant, and of my wife and child. But most of all, lover of my harmless and sanguine self."

When I think of the word *overture*, two things come to mind. An overture is an introduction to something more substantial. An overture also connotes music. Beginning with an overture requires both. Hansen and Hawkes give us these overtures before they tell us what their stories are. And they do it lyrically. The writing is musical. If it wasn't, these opening paragraphs would read like two long lists.

Otherworld

GREGOR SAMSA WAKES up and discovers he's a giant cockroach in the first line of Franz Kafka's *The Metamorphosis*. On a cold day in April, the clocks strike thirteen in George Orwell's *1984*. These beginnings tell the reader right away that he or she is entering a world that is different than his or her own. By opening like this, the writer—and the world created—gain authority. Samsa *is* a cockroach. The clocks *are* striking thirteen.

Joseph Conrad said that writing is creating worlds. Kafka and Orwell are literally creating different worlds—worlds in which a man can wake up a cockroach or in which there is a thirteen o'clock. But really, every writer creates a new world every time he or she begins a new story, and from the very beginning, the writer needs to establish the rules of that world. In *Mrs.*

Dalloway, we enter a world in which Clarissa Dalloway decides to buy the flowers herself. In *Anna Karenina,* we enter a world in which unhappy families are all different in their own way. No matter how you decide to begin your novel, that beginning brings the reader into a world of your own making.

One of my favorite first lines in recent literature is the first line of *Middlesex* by Jeffrey Eugenides: "I was born twice: first, as a baby girl, on a remarkably smogless Detroit day in January of 1960; and then again, as a teenage boy, in an emergency room near Petoskey, Michigan, in August of 1974." In this beginning, Eugenides creates an otherworld, one in which the protagonist is born twice. He gives us facts—dates, places. He uses setting—a remarkably smogless day, an emergency room near Petoskey. And the protagonist introduces himself by telling us, "I was born twice."

But most importantly, this beginning—like every one I've mentioned and every one in those books on your bookshelves—is so well written, so fresh and compelling that it makes me want to read more. Isn't that really all that a good beginning needs to do?

DON'T WRITE WHAT YOU KNOW

BRET ANTHONY JOHNSTON

EVERY WEDNESDAY, I teach an introductory fiction workshop at Harvard University, and on the first day of class I pass out a bulleted list of things the students should try hard to avoid. Don't start a story with an alarm clock going off. Don't end a story with the whole shebang having been a suicide note. Don't use flashy dialogue tags like *intoned* or *queried* or, God forbid, *ejaculated*. Twelve unbearably gifted students are sitting around the table, and they appreciate having such parameters established. With each variable the list isolates, their imaginations soar higher. They smile and nod. The mood in the room is congenial, almost festive with learning. I feel like a very effective teacher; I can practically hear my course-evaluation scores hitting the roof. Then, when the students reach the last point on the list, the mood shifts. Some of them squint at the words as if their vision has gone blurry; others ask their neighbors for clarification. The neighbor will shake her head, looking pale and dejected, as if the last point confirms that she should have opted for that aseptic-surgery class in which you operate on a fetal pig. The last point is "Don't Write What You Know."

The idea panics them for two reasons. First, like all writers, the students have been encouraged, explicitly or implicitly, for as long as they can remember, to write what they know, so the prospect of abandoning that approach now is disorienting. Second, they know an awful lot. In recent workshops, my students have included Iraq War veterans, professional athletes, a minister, a circus clown, a woman with a pet miniature elephant, and gobs of certified geniuses. They are endlessly interesting people, their lives brimming with uniquely compelling experiences, and too often they believe those experiences are what equip them to be writers. Encouraging them not to write what they know sounds as wrongheaded as a football coach telling a quarterback with a bazooka of a right arm to ride the bench. For them, the advice is confusing and heartbreaking, maybe even insulting. For me, it's the difference between fiction that matters only to those who know the author and fiction that, well, matters.

IN THE SPIRIT of full disclosure, I should admit I've been accused of writing what I know on a good many occasions. Acquaintances, book reviewers, kind souls who've attended public readings, students, they've all charged me with writing autobiographical fiction. Sometimes, the critic notes a parallel between my background and that of a character. At other times, the reasoning is fuzzier. A woman at a reading once told me, "I liked your book a lot, but the stories made me think you'd be taller." I'm never offended; at times, I've been weirdly flattered. Comments like these make me think I'm getting away with something.

The facts are these: I was born and raised in Corpus Christi, Texas, the part of the country where most every word of fiction I've published takes place. I grew up around horses and hurricanes; my father worried about money, occasionally moonlighted to pay the bills, and died young; my mother smoked and paid mightily for it. If you read *Corpus Christi: Stories*, you'll undoubtedly recognize elements from my life; however, very few of the experiences in the book are my own. In early versions of some stories, my impulse was to try to record how certain events in my life had played out, but by the third draft, I was prohibitively bored. I knew how, in real life, the stories ended, and I had a pretty firm idea of what they "meant," so the story could not surprise me or provide an opportunity for wonder. I was writing to explain, not to discover. The writing process was as exciting as completing a crossword puzzle I'd already solved. So I changed my approach.

Instead of thinking of my experiences as structures I wanted to erect in fiction, I started conceiving of them as the scaffolding that would be torn down once the work was complete. I took small details from my life to evoke a place and the people who inhabit it, but those details served only to illuminate my imagination. Previously, I'd forced my fiction to conform to the contours of my life; now I sought out any and every point where a plot could be rerouted from what I'd known. The shift was seismic. My confidence waned, but my curiosity sprawled. I had been writing fiction, to paraphrase William Trevor, not to express myself, but to escape myself. When I recall those stories now, the flashes of autobiography remind me of stars staking a constellation. Individually, the stars are unimportant; only when they map shapes in the darkness, shapes born of imagination, do we understand their light.

I DON'T KNOW the origin of the "Write What You Know" logic. A lot of folks attribute it to Hemingway, but what I find is his having said this: "From all things that you know and all those you cannot know, you make something through your invention that is not a representation but a whole new thing truer than anything true and alive." If this is the logic's origin, then maybe what's happened is akin to that old game called Telephone. In the game, one kid whispers a message to a second kid, then that kid whispers it to a third, and so on, until the message circles the room and returns to the first kid. The message is always altered, minimized, and corrupted by translation. "Bill is smart to sit in the grass" becomes "Bill is a smart-ass." A similar transmission problem undermines the logic of writing what you know and, ironically, Hemingway may have been arguing against it all along. The very act of committing an experience to the page is necessarily an act of reduction, and regardless of craft or skill, vision or voice, the result is a story beholden to and inevitably eclipsed by source material.

Another confession: part of me dies inside when a student whose story has been critiqued responds to the workshop by saying, "You can't object to the _____ scene. It really happened! I was there!" The writer is giving preference to the facts of an experience, the so-called literal truth, rather than fiction's narrative and emotional integrity. Conceived this way, the writer's story is relegated to an inferior and insurmountable station; it can neither compete with nor live without the ur-experience.

Such a writer's sole ambition is for the characters and events to *represent* other and superior—i.e., actual—characters and events. Meaning, the written story has never been what mattered most. Meaning, the reader is intended to care less about the characters and more about whoever inspired them, and the actions in a story serve to ensure that we track their provenance and regard that material as truer. Meaning, the story is engineered—and expected—to be *about* something. And aboutness is all but terminal in fiction.

Stories aren't about things. Stories *are* things.

Stories aren't about actions. Stories are, unto themselves, actions.

LET ME BE perfectly clear: I don't tell students *not* to ferret through their lives for potential stories. I don't want, say, a soldier who served in Iraq to shy away from writing war stories. Quite the opposite. I want him to freight his fiction with rich details of combat. I want the story to evoke the texture of the sand and the noise of a Baghdad bazaar, the terrible and beautiful shade of blue smoke ribboning from the barrel of his M4. His experience should liberate his imagination, not restrict it. Of course I want him to take inspiration where he can find it. What I don't want—and what's prone to happen when writers set out to write what they know—is for him to think an imagined story is less urgent, less harrowing or authentic, than a true story.

Take, for example, *The Lazarus Project*, by Bosnian-born author Aleksandar Hemon. In this superb and wrenching novel, Hemon entwines two narratives—the 1908 murder of Lazarus Averbuch in Chicago and the present-day journey of a writer named Brik through Eastern Europe to research a book about Lazarus. Superficially, the novel seems as entrenched in autobiography as it is in history: Brik, like Hemon, was born in Bosnia, and Hemon lives, like the fictional Brik, in Chicago; Hemon, like Brik, also traveled through Europe to research the project with a photographer friend, and sure enough, both a photographer friend and photographs can be found in the novel. However, *The Lazarus Project* is far more than the sum of its parts. The raw materials serve Hemon's fiction in the same way that paint, canvas, and onions served Cezanne's *Still Life with Onions*. The goal isn't to represent an experience, but instead to create a piece of art that is itself an experience. In a recent interview, Hemon, a MacArthur "genius grant" recipient, said, "I reserve the right to get engaged with any aspect of human experience, and so that means that I can—indeed I must—go beyond my experience to engage. That's non-negotiable." Amen.

And what of Lorrie Moore's masterpiece "People Like That Are the Only People Here: Canonical Babbling in Peed Onk"? Upon its publication in 1997, many readers assumed Moore's short story of parents coping with their one-year-old boy's kidney cancer was nonfiction; after all, her family had endured a similar trauma, and the mother in the story was, like Moore, a teacher and fiction writer. (At one point, the father encourages the mother to "take notes" on the ordeal so she can write and sell a story to offset the mounting medical expenses.) And yet the story's potency is attributable to the architecture of fiction, the distance that Moore pries open between her family and the family on the page. A straightforward recounting of the experience would merely confirm what reader and author already know:

cancer is horrible, watching children suffer is horrible, et cetera. To affect the reader, to reveal the fullness and force of such trauma, Moore invokes her imagination. She deploys humor, wordplay, dramatized scenes, a complex (mostly) third-person narration, and an apparatus of irony built on the crucial conceit that the mother lacks the necessary skill and courage to write this story. As she makes her way to see her son after his surgery, her thinking sums up the limitations of simply writing what you know: "How can any of it be described? The trip and the story of the trip are always two different things . . . One cannot go to a place and speak of it; one cannot both see and say, not really."

Or, speaking of war stories, consider Tim O'Brien's collection, *The Things They Carried*. The book renders the myriad horrors, exhilarations, doldrums, and tragedies of the Vietnam War with vividness and intimacy, and because the author is a veteran, the book's power might be assumed to emanate from O'Brien's firsthand knowledge. And maybe it does. But in "Good Form," one of the short-short stories in the collection, the narrator says, "Story-truth is truer sometimes than happening-truth." I've always found an abiding comfort in this claim, and the comfort is compounded by the fact that the narrator is a man who shares so much of the author's pedigree—his experience in Vietnam, his current literary vocation, even his age and name. O'Brien could have written the "happening-truth" of his experience and called it a day. (In fact, he did just that in his first book, *If I Die in a Combat Zone, Box Me Up and Ship Me Home*.) But by choosing fiction here, especially after having written a nonfiction account of his experiences, he tacitly acknowledges that something is gained by setting imagination loose on history, something profound and revelatory and vital: empathy. Empathy, to my mind, is the channel through which writer and reader can most assuredly connect with the characters. And if personal experience constrains a story, often to the point of dullness and abstraction, then empathy simultaneously sharpens and emancipates it. O'Brien writes:

> Here is happening-truth, I was once a soldier. There were many bodies, real bodies with real faces, but I was young then and afraid to look . . .
>
> Here is the story-truth. He was a slim, dead, almost dainty young man of about twenty. He lay in the center of a red clay trail near the village of My Khe. His jaw was in his throat. His one eye was shut, the other eye was a star-shaped hole. I killed him.

ANOTHER DEEPER, MORE essential part of me dies when a workshop student says, "What I wanted to do was _____." The idea of a writer "wanting" to do something in a story unhinges me. At best, such desire smacks of nostalgia; at worst, it betrays agenda. I feel pity for the characters, a real sense of futility. I'm reminded of Ron Carlson's hilarious story "What We Wanted to Do," in which a group of villagers intends to spill a cauldron of boiling oil on the Visigoths storming their gates. The oil, however, never reaches its boiling point, so when the villagers commence their dousing, the liquid is lukewarm and the Visigoths aren't so much scalded as they are terribly pissed off. The result is their most vicious attack. The lesson is a good one for fiction writers: stories fueled by intentions never reach their boiling point.

And writing what you know *is* knotted up with intention, and intention in fiction is always related to control, to rigidity, and, more often than not, to a little solipsism. The writer seems to have chosen an event because it illustrates a point or mounts an argument. When a fiction writer has a message to deliver, a residue of smugness is often in the prose, a distressing sense of the story's being rushed, of the author's going through the motions, hurrying the characters toward whatever wisdom awaits on the last page. As a reader, I feel pandered to and closed out. Maybe even a little bullied. My involvement in the story, like the characters', becomes utterly passive. We are there to follow orders, to admire and applaud the author's supposed insight.

MAYBE, THOUGH, THE hardest thing for me to hear in workshop is a student's claim that he isn't "comfortable" writing certain stories. The words are almost blasphemous to me, equally saddening and maddening. Usually, the student's discomfort relates to race or gender, sexuality or class. He feels ill-equipped to write about characters that don't resemble him in the mirror and the bedroom, so he reverts to writing what he knows. I argue that if the subject or character is intimidating, then that's exactly what the writer should be exploring in fiction. My students worry about being invasive or predatory, and few things frighten them more than charges of appropriation and literary trespassing. But I see an altogether more menacing threat: the devaluing not only of imagination but also of compassion. And if empathy is important to fiction, compassion is invaluable. Compassion is empathy on steroids.

Was Toni Morrison a slave? Did she ever slit a child's throat? Was Nabokov, in light of his "fancy prose style," a murderer? Has Haruki Murakami ever constructed a flute from the souls of cats? Yes, Flannery O'Connor limped, but did she ever lose a wooden leg to a huckster Bible salesman? Tim O'Brien served in Vietnam, but, as the narrator of "Good Form" says, "almost everything else is invented." Even without extended research, I can guarantee Ron Carlson has never spilled oil onto the head of a Visigoth.

ALL OF THIS recalls for me an interview with Allan Gurganus, the sublime novelist who so thoroughly imagined Lucy Marsden, that oldest living Confederate widow who dished all her secrets. Gurganus says, "As an amateur historian, I'm forever aware that 'the second story' of a building once referred to its murals." I also remember reading that the murals painted on a building's interior walls usually depicted a tale from history, and thus, if you were on the fourth floor, if you were seeing the fourth mural, you were on the fourth *story*. In the interview, Gurganus goes on to say, "For fantasists like me, history constitutes the ground floor only, staff entrance. We all enter there but—given our spirit yearnings, our malformed characters, as soon as possible, we ascend." This seems inviolably true to me, and impossibly inspiring. Writers may enter their stories through literal experience, through the ground floor, but fiction brings with it an obligation to rise past the base level, to transcend the limitations of fact and history, and proceed skyward.

I'm also thinking again about my fiction workshop, those Wednesdays spent talking about people who don't exist, and how chilled the students are when I discourage them from writing what they know. To reanimate them—or at least salvage my course-evaluation scores—I say fiction is an act of courage and humility, a protest against our mortality, and we, the authors, don't matter. What matters are our characters, those constructions of imagination that can transcend our biases and agendas, our egos and entitlements and flesh. Trust your powers of empathy and invention, I say. Trust the example of the authors you love to read—as Flaubert said, "Emma, *c'est moi*"—and trust that your craft, when braided with compassion, will produce stories that matter both to you and to readers you've never met.

The students mostly buy it. Week by week, their stories are arresting and rewarding, and with each revision, I feel more optimistic, more reassured and moved by their work. My students succeed about as often as most writers do, as often as I do—in other words, often enough. As I read their good fiction, though, I sometimes wonder if I haven't misunderstood something simple and essential. I've long believed that what keeps writers—again, myself included—from fully transcending their personal experiences on the page is fear of incompetence: I can't write a plot that involves a kidnapping because I've never been kidnapped. But what if it's the opposite? What if the reason we find it so difficult to cleave our fiction from our experience, the reason we're so loath to engage our imaginations and let the story rise above the ground floor of truth, isn't that we're afraid we'll do the job poorly but that we're afraid we'll do it too well? If we succeed, if the characters are fully imagined, if they are so beautifully real that they quicken and rise off the page, then maybe our own experiences will feel smaller, our actions less consequential. Maybe we're afraid that if we write what we don't know, we'll discover something truer than anything our real lives will ever yield. And maybe we'll encounter still another, more insidious threat—the threat that if we do our jobs too well, if we powerfully render characters who are untethered from our experience, they'll supplant us in the reader's mind. Maybe we worry that fiction's vividness will put our own brief and negligible lives into too stark a relief, and the reader, seduced by literature's permanence, will leave us behind. Maybe we worry we'll be forgotten. Maybe we're afraid of what we want most—for our characters to outlive us—and maybe the possibility that the writer, not the reader, will get lost in the pages of a great book is, ultimately, too much for us to bear.

FUNNY IS THE NEW DEEP:

An Exploration of the Comic Impulse

STEVE ALMOND

MOST PEOPLE'S FIRST formal introduction to what I'll be calling, for the purpose of this essay, "the comic impulse" arrives via Aristotle. Good old Aristotle! So wise. So Greek. So hot.

In his *Poetics*, Aristotle writes about four modes of literature: the tragic, the epic, the lyric, and the comic. As useful as this taxonomy might be in some respects, it has led to a vague consensus that the tragic and comic modes of literature are not only distinct but diametrically opposed. This notion is complete nonsense. In fact, the comic impulse almost always arises directly from our efforts to contend with tragedy. It is the safest and most reliable way to acknowledge our circumstances without being crushed by them.

Writers in the early stages of their apprenticeship tend to look down upon the comic impulse. I certainly did. Back in the midnineties, when I was excreting my earliest drafts, I wanted, more than anything, to be taken seriously. If enough people took me seriously I might start to take myself seriously, thereby dispelling the notion, forever lurking at the gates of ambition, that I was a sad clown who should quit writing and return to my given career as a professional masturbator, a career for which I am even now somewhat nostalgic. Big awards, and the vengeful omnipotence that goes along with them, were handed out to folks like Hemingway and Faulkner, who did not smile, let alone crack wise. This mind-set spurred the production of many serious, high-minded, earnest, and almost inevitably dreary pieces of short fiction intended to prove my good habits of thought and feeling. I really was a nice Jewish boy from the suburbs, very clean, very obedient, very *serious*.

To me, back then, perhaps as to you, here and now, the "comic impulse" meant a conscious desire to be funny, to entertain people, to make them laugh. I can assure you that the absolute worst way to pursue a career making people laugh is to set out to be funny. It doesn't work that way. On the contrary, comedy is produced by a determined confrontation with a set of feeling states that are essentially tragic in nature: grief, shame, disappointment, physical discomfort, anxiety, moral outrage. It is not about pleasing the reader. It's about purging the writer.

Another way of saying this would be that the best comedy is rooted in the capacity to face unbearable emotions and to offer, by means of laughter, a dividend of forgiveness. Sometimes, these emotions have to do with the world around us. For the most part, they have to do with the world inside us.

Let me offer, as evidence, a quick and embarrassingly spotty survey of the relevant literature.

Consider the Greek playwright Aristophanes, who died two years before Aristotle was born. He is sometimes called the Father of Comedy, which is absurd, given that comedy has been around for as long as people, or primates, have been taking pratfalls. His satires not only provide us with a vivid portrait of ancient Athens, they also constitute a concerted effort to confront the hypocrisy and corruption of his government. Jon Stewart owes Aristophanes plenty.

Cervante's *Don Quixote*, by acclaim our first great novel, is a comic picaresque triggered by obsessive disappointment and driven along not by heroic action, but by humiliation. Dante's *Divine Comedy* was written, in part, as an expression of the author's volcanic rage at having been exiled from his beloved Florence. Shakespeare's comedies can be seen as sustained and often ruthless examinations of various species of human folly. And so on and so on, from *Tristram Shandy* to *Huck Finn* to *Lucky Jim* to *The Catcher in the Rye* to *Infinite Jest*.

Embedded within all these texts is the following nifty irony: the comic impulse is simultaneously an expression of helplessness, of surrender to the world's absurd cruelty and our own foibles and fuckups, *and* the acquisition of power by means of acknowledging that bad data.

Consider, for example, the landscape of *King Lear*: the one character vested with the power to speak truth to the king is the Fool. Now think about the first mass-media figure to confront the atrocities of fascism: Charlie Chaplin. He made *The Great Dictator* in 1940, when the United States was formally at peace with Nazi Germany. Chaplin excoriated the Nazis as "machine men, with machine minds and machine hearts."

Two of the greatest American novels ever written—certainly the two greatest to emerge from World War II—are both comedies: *Catch-22* by Joseph Heller and *Slaughterhouse Five* by Kurt Vonnegut. A few years ago, I had the privilege of looking through Vonnegut's papers, which are archived at Indiana University in Bloomington, Indiana. People often forget this, but Vonnegut spent more than two decades trying to write *Slaughterhouse Five*. Like most young writers, he was determined to be taken seriously, and he took his topic to be of the utmost gravity, and this meant, to him, that he was duty bound to write a series of serious, well-meaning, and ultimately dreary short stories. The only cool thing about reading these stories was that they afforded me the chance to realize that Kurt Vonnegut's prose once sucked—always an exhilarating realization for envious little strivers like myself.

These stories, by the way, contain many of the events that would later appear in *Slaughterhouse Five*, and even some of the character names. Yet they are terse, competent, lifeless. He'd clearly been mainlining Hemingway, or early Mailer.

It took Vonnegut years to locate the voice he needed to tell the story of his experiences as a POW during the bombing of Dresden. And if you read the introduction to the novel, one of the greatest pieces of writing he ever produced, what you hear in his tone is essentially surrender. Surrender to the absurd. Surrender to the human capacity for senseless cruelty. Surrender to his own literary inadequacies. He writes:

> I would hate to tell you what this lousy little book cost me in money and anxiety and time. When I got home from the Second World War twenty three years ago, I thought it would be easy for me to write about the destruction of Dresden, since

all I would have to do would be to report what I had seen. And I thought, too, that it would be a masterpiece or at least make me a lot of money, since the subject was so big.

But not many words about Dresden came from my mind then—not enough of them to make a book, anyway. And not many words come now, either, when I have become an old fart with his memories and his Pall Malls, with his sons full grown.

What's so fascinating—and revealing—is that this voice isn't something he had to create. It was already inside him. The most telling document in that entire archive is the letter Vonnegut wrote to his family on May 29, 1945, from a repatriation camp in Le Havre, France, literally days after he'd been liberated: "I'm told that you were probably never informed that I was anything other than 'missing in action,'" he begins. "That leaves me a lot of explaining to do . . . On about February 14th the Americans came over, followed by the R.A.F. Their combined labors killed [25,000] people in twenty-four hours and destroyed all of Dresden—possibly the world's most beautiful city. But not me."

Can you hear that? *That* is Vonnegut's voice, that fearless, mordant surrender to the absurd. It was inside of him all that time. And it's inside of you, too. Every single person has a distinct sense of humor that allows him or her to speak more truthfully, that allows him or her to draw closer to the eternal flame of sorrow than most—if not all!—of the other voices at your disposal.

Because the comic impulse, it turns out, isn't a literary device at all. It's a bioevolutionary adaptation. It's a survival mechanism human beings developed to contend with the perils of self-consciousness and moral awareness, as well as with the horrible outcomes they needed to be able to imagine to ensure their survival on the mean streets of the Serengeti or the Neander Valley.

What's my point? That, sometimes, atrocity is the midwife of the comic? Without the atrocity of slavery, Mark Twain never writes *The Adventures of Huckleberry Finn*? Actually, I think I'm saying just the opposite, too. The comic impulse is what allows us to recognize our sins (personal, cultural, historical) and thereby make moral progress. Great comic writers recognize, in a way that most of us can't or won't, that our moral universe is out of balance, that the king is crazy, the dictator is mad—that we're in a lot of trouble.

This has never been more true than today, which is why the most cogent moral watchdogs—as our Fourth Estate descends into a kind of regressed capitalist psychosis—are all comedians. Lenny Bruce begets Richard Pryor, who begets Bill Hicks, who begets Jon Stewart and Bill Maher. Vonnegut begets George Saunders and Lorrie Moore and Sam Lipsyte.

Another way of thinking about all this is that the comic impulse is what allows us to confront cruelty. It allows us to speak in explicit moral terms, without moralizing. It allows us to take direct aim at the sponsors of cruelty, because, hey, we're just the fool. George W. Bush's saggy white ass, meet Stephen Colbert's mighty boot of truth. *Good evening, Mr. President, I'd like to begin by saying you're just a pathetic rich boy who likes to dress up like GI Joe and sodomize the poor. Just kidding. Ha. Ha. Ha.*

It's worth noting here that one of the most troubling symptoms of the right wing of this country—along with an energetic aptitude for violence, projection, and toddler logic—is that it has no sense of humor whatsoever. Because a sense of humor implies a basic recognition, if not a celebration, of moral uncertainty and confusion. What the voices of the right deal in, their essential commodity, is moral surety, the trademark of the demented. The narrative of the right in this country is deeply rooted in a feverish denial of reality: greed is not snuffing out generosity, the planet isn't heating up, our corporations will care for us, America remains the greatest country on earth, just so long as we can get those poverty-stricken undocumented gay Communist academics to shut the fuck up. The right wing runs on rage, which is the fuel of convenience when you run out of truth.

But the confrontation I keep talking about need not be with the external world of corruption. Just as often—more often, actually—it's a confrontation with the internal world. In this personal sense, the comic impulse consists of an articulation of private, shameful, and, above all, transgressive thoughts.

The writer Luis Urrea recently spoke to this with great eloquence in a craft talk. He said, "All the embarrassing things that I talk about—being from Tijuana, being poor, having contracted tuberculosis—are the ones that deeply affect people." In other words, the comic impulse, that essential surrender to the absurdity of the universe, is what allows him to speak about this painful stuff. Like a good Catholic boy—or maybe a bad Catholic boy, I honestly don't know enough about Catholicism to say— Urrea is seeking to confess and to forgive himself all at once. His jokes are the confession and our laughter is the forgiveness.

The comic impulse, then, is about a willingness to dwell in the awkward, shameful places we'd prefer not to dwell. It's what allows us to face the truth of ourselves on behalf of others. I often tell students that the path to the truth runs through shame. But it's equally important to note that you sometimes need the cloak of humor to get yourself into, and through, the darkest parts of the forest.

The idea isn't to crack jokes about your life. On the contrary, the idea is to engage in a ruthless pursuit of the truth, and to allow the comic impulse to do its intended and instinctual work. It's not some wrench you hoist out of your writer's toolbox when the action seems to be flagging. It's the impulse that naturally arises when you reach a moment that is too painful to confront without some form of self-forgiveness. It's not a conscious decision, but an unconscious necessity.

And this applies, by the way, to fiction and nonfiction and poetry. Every time I reach a point of unbearable heaviness in one of my stories or essays or rotten novels, my natural inclination is to offer some form of comic relief. In initial drafts, this desire to "joke around" is often an evasive tactic, and these are the jokes I wind up cutting later, the moments that arise from a desire to elide the truth or to please the reader and thereby flatter myself. But the jokes that my characters require, in order to face the truth of themselves and their circumstances—those are the ones that stay.

Honestly, this is just human nature. We all grew up in families that were screwed up in various innovative ways, and we all developed, as a coping mechanism, a sense of humor. To reiterate, your sense of humor did not begin as a narrative strategy, but as an adaptive instinct. And that's what it should remain in your work. The idea is not to hide behind a set of jokes, but to relax sufficiently so as to allow for some play, some improvisation, at the keyboard. Self-consciousness is the death of art, as John Cage reminds us. Taking yourself, or your characters, too seriously is as grave a danger as taking them too lightly. When the stink of gravity grows thick upon your keyboard, let humor be your aromatherapy.

I am sometimes asked what I think is funny. This is mostly an issue of comic sensibility, of personal inclination. My daughter and I, for instance, find the concept of poopie soup to be extremely funny. Sometimes we stir the poopie soup. Sometimes we pretend to sniff, or even taste, the poopie soup, then recoil in delighted horror. My wife, sadly, does not appreciate the comedic genius of poopie soup. Am I suggesting my wife has a bad sense of humor? Yes. On the other hand, in this matter at least, she feels I have a bad sense of humor. Everyone responds to a different soup.

But I will say a few things that I think apply across the board. Something is funny, most of all, because it's true, and because the velocity of insight into this truth exceeds our normal standards. Something is funny because it's outside our accepted boundary of decorum. Something is funny because it defies our expectations. Something is funny because it offers a temporary reprieve from the hardship of seeing the world as it actually is. Something is funny because it is able to suggest gently that even the worst of our circumstances and sins is subject to eventual mercy. There are different sorts of laughter, in other words, and they express varying degrees of joy, affirmation, surprise, and relief.

The comic impulse is, in essence, a form of radicalism. To put it in psychoanalytic terms, it's an attempt to turn away from the safety of our superegos and unchain the raging, anarchic id that yearns to be free. It's the force that allows well-behaved Philip Roth to escape from the comfy confines of *Goodbye, Columbus* for the libidinal jungle of *Portnoy's Complaint*.

I think now of one of my Boston College students, a young man who was not named Matt or Ryan, or Matt Ryan, as so many BC dudes are. No, his name was Pete. He was in the first humor writing class I ever taught. I had assumed this would be a very easy class to teach, because college students are constantly insecure and therefore constantly talking shit about the world around them and all I had to do was get them to talk shit onto the page.

Instead, I received a raft of safe, well-meaning satires meant to condemn the horrors of racism, sexism, and excluding a particular suitemate because she still wore Uggs. A month into class, I convened a come-to-Jesus meeting. "Listen," I said. "I'm not interested in your good values. They bore me. You are boring me to death. If I receive another earnest, obedient word from anyone in this class, so help me God, I will flunk every one of your sorry asses. I'm a fucking adjunct. I can do it."

The next class, Pete brought in a piece on shitting in public. It was a long and detailed primer that introduced the reader to terms such as "the half-crap" and "prairie-dogging." Wow. That class was really an excruciating and deeply awesome fifty minutes of life. Because, after all, one of the containing myths of collegiate life (and maybe life in general) is that women do not defecate. But the piece was so extreme, and so courageous in confronting the most private of our fundamental bodily shames, that it really broke the class open.

It might be said that these students had been given permission to play with their own shit. We are all seeking, on some deeper spiritual level, permission to play with our own shit, to unburden ourselves of the strangling illusion that we are somehow not a total mess. Remember: we all have a sense of humor by which we've survived the worst moments of our lives, and forgiven ourselves at various wretched junctures.

The real question isn't whether you can or should try to be funny in your work, but whether you're going to get yourself and your characters into enough danger to invoke the comic impulse. Literary artists don't write funny to produce laughter—though we're certainly thrilled when people laugh—but to apprehend and endure the astonishing sorrow of the examined life.

RESEARCH IN FICTION

ANDREA BARRETT

I LOVE RESEARCH, in all its aspects. I love trolling for material in libraries and rummage sales and people's basements, at antiquarian bookshops and in old encyclopedias. I love the dusty shelves, the foxed pages smelling of mildew, the excitement of following through book after book a trail that makes sense only to me.

Research has led me to odd places: Once, for a story called "Theories of Rain," I read about the history of meteorology, especially early ideas about the formation of dew and rain and clouds; about John and William Bartram, two American botanists who lived outside of Philadelphia during the eighteenth and early nineteenth centuries; about the travels of Peter Kalm, who was a student of Linnaeus; about what kinds of plants composed an early nineteenth-century hay field; about the role of women in early childhood education and the history of textbook publication. Another time, a long rampage through the history of utopian communities—in particular the one at New Harmony—set me to investigating the many early American naturalists who'd been involved with that place and then to a crucial moment in the history of paleontology when the fossils people were finding in the ground were suddenly seen to be evidence that the earth might not have been created in six days, but could instead be immeasurably older. As the story eventually called "Two Rivers" grew, I learned about the physical and economic conditions in early nineteenth-century Pittsburgh; migration along the Ohio River valley; the differing construction of keelboats and flatboats; the history of the education of the deaf; and what was in a pharmacist's shop around 1825. By the time I was done, the character with whom I'd started had evolved so unexpectedly that he never reached New Harmony at all.

Similarly, work on a story called "Servants of the Map" meant learning from scratch what my chief character, Max, might have seen and felt during his travels in the Himalayan region, about which I knew nothing. Along the way, I investigated the history of the British rule of India and the 1857 mutiny there; Himalayan exploration; the life of the British botanist Joseph Dalton Hooker; nineteenth-century Kashmir and its conflicts with India; the botany of the Karakoram region; and Asa Gray's role in bringing Darwin's conception of evolution to the United States. As often happens—because all of that, as useful as it was, still couldn't tell me what Max had *felt*—the reading led me back out into the world. Wanting something more than my own modest experience of hiking and climbing in the mountains, something closer to what Max had done, I visited the area around Lake Louise in western Canada. At the Athabasca glacier, a nice young man who makes his living guiding people obligingly roped me up and lowered me down a crevasse. I was perfectly safe, strapped into a harness, clinging to a rope that wound through pulleys and ice screws and all sorts of paraphernalia. The crevasse wasn't very big; I was less than a mile from the highway; I was hanging only twenty feet down. But that was enough for me to see something I'd never read about: the two sides of the crevasse have completely different textures—an intense sensual image that I *couldn't* gain from a book.

These sense perceptions always seem like doors, to me—the right one will help me imagine myself into an entirely different time and place. Even though I'd never climbed above twelve thousand feet or fallen into a glacier, and couldn't in a million years have hauled myself out of this one, the sensation of dangling between two walls of ice, with only a slot of sky over my head, stayed with me and illuminated the rest of my reading. Similarly, having had altitude sickness a few times myself helped me sense, when reading the work of mountaineers writing in earlier centuries, what a much worse version of that felt like to them.

These are ridiculous examples, I know; writing is often ridiculous. Still, all of it—the reading, the modest outdoor adventures, the unexpected conversations (once, for instance, I went to a small, old-fashioned museum in Cambridge to see the fossils collected by the geologist Adam Sedgwick, and found in addition the shy and elderly curator who knew the provenance of every stone and fossil in his care, and who told me wonderful stories)—every bit of it, has been rewarding.

But. But.

I hate how dangerous research can be for our work. It's always easier, and often more fun, to dive into books and photos and the shark-filled depths of the online world than to write. It's delightful to learn new things. It's delicious to uncover buried connections and make links that we think haven't been made before. And it's tempting—*so* tempting; you can walk into any bookstore and put your hand on twenty volumes plagued by this—to take everything we've learned and dump it, untransformed, onto the page. To stuff in all we've found, emptying the file of notes in an effort not to "waste" all the hard work.

You know the result: a kind of horrible Jell-O mold, flabby lime green prose heavily studded with the cubed canned peaches and maraschino cherries of trivial fact. In place of complex characters and living language, detailed descriptions of streetlights and women's clothes and plumbing, stick figures quoting pages from newspapers, dinner discussions during which national boundaries are decided. The research connected neither to the characters nor to their emotions; the characters themselves mere mouthpieces for exposition, camera lenses for the recording of travelogue-ish impressions; weird tonal issues, ranging from a reverential hush that strangles all life to a cynical knowingness. Wink-wink, nudge-nudge, see how wrongheaded those people were! How silly, compared to our own advanced state!

It's easy to blame our reliance on Google and Wikipedia for this—it was harder to go quite so wrong in the days when research meant heading into a library and laboriously taking notes for months. We don't write down everything we read; note taking means selecting, which already implies active understanding and judgment, which cuts down the clutter. But a Wikipedia entry can be copied with a click, then inserted with another directly into whatever we're writing—and in some heavily researched fiction, that feels like exactly what's happened. Still, the fault is ours; the technology only makes it easier to misunderstand what the research is *for*, and easier to write fiction that apes history or biography without adding anything: history-lite, biography-lite.

So then why, given all these perils, might we *want* to use research in our fiction? The simplest answer is that our own lives are limited and, for all but the most Proustian among us, finite as a source for fiction. Exceptionally beautiful books have been made by writers drawing exclusively on autobiographical material—but for most of us, that well eventually runs dry. Some writers cease to write then, after one or two books. Others repeat themselves. A happier choice is to draw on the enormous richness of the world around us. Research, especially when approached in a spirit of play and open-mindedness, offers access to all the lives we haven't lived, aren't living, probably won't live. It's a way of making things we sometimes don't think of as material for fiction—science and medicine, for example—available to us. And it's also a way of sinking into the hearts and minds of our characters.

As long as our research feeds what we're actually writing and is transformed by embodying it in story and scene, we may find a home for things that at first seem disparate, but actually aren't. We know all sorts of things—what we've brushed up against in the course of daily existence, and bits of what our friends and lovers and colleagues and acquaintances and neighbors know, and things overheard at a party, and other things we've heard on the radio or read, in addition to all we actively seek to learn. If we let our own curiosity and the curiosity of our characters guide us, following the needs of the fiction evolving on the page, those unexpected conjunctions can enrich our fiction and lead us into new and fruitful areas. The worst difficulties seem to arise when we do all our research *before* writing, studiously heading down a predetermined path, along a line of argument or inquiry we've determined intellectually, and then shaping our characters and stories to fit what we've found.

The question we have to keep asking ourselves is, What is the research *for*? Think about this: research is simply a way of *understanding what our characters understand*. No less than that; but also no more. Not what people later thought, after consideration and analysis, about the events through which our characters pass, but what our characters knew and saw and read and felt as they were living the moments they were living. It doesn't do the writing any good to understand *analytically* a huge amount about the world our characters inhabit. What helps is to understand what their world *feels* like, *looks* like: sensual details, images charged with emotion. We both can't and shouldn't use a tenth of what we find, and in our final drafts we'll end up cutting much of what we did first use. But in the process of the research we may, ideally, be able to feel ourselves into the state of our characters.

For a little reinforcement here, I'm going to turn to an essay Marguerite Yourcenar wrote about the composition of her novel *Memoirs of Hadrian*. She says:

Those who put the historical novel in a category apart are forgetting that what every novelist does is only to interpret, by means of the techniques which his period affords, a certain number of past events; his memories, whether consciously or unconsciously recalled, whether personal or impersonal, are all woven of the same stuff as History itself. . . .

48

We lose track of everything, and of everyone, even ourselves. The facts of my father's life are less known to me than
those of the life of Hadrian. My own existence, if I had to write
of it, would be reconstructed by me from externals, laboriously,
as if it were the life of someone else: I should have to turn to
letters, and to the recollections of others, in order to clarify such
uncertain memories. What is ever left but crumbled walls, or
masses of shade? . . .

The rules of the game: learn everything, read everything,
inquire into everything, while at the same time adapting to
one's ends the *Spiritual Exercises* of Ignatius of Loyola, or the
method of Hindu ascetics, who for years, and to the point of
exhaustion, try to visualize ever more exactly the images which
they create beneath their closed eyelids."[1]

I like the way Yourcenar reminds us that while fiction based
on research poses its own problems, many of those problems are
common at a deep level to *any* fiction. Research serves fiction
best when it's dissolved entirely into the work, reprecipitated
only to be embodied in characters, images, and the sensual details bringing the scene alive for the characters and hence for us.
Research serves fiction best when it transcends the given facts
and moves into the realm of the imagination.

Willa Cather, often a touchstone for me in these matters, offers
this in her essay "The Novel Démeublé": "If the novel is a form of
imaginative art, it cannot be at the same time a vivid and brilliant
form of journalism. Out of the teeming, gleaming stream of the
present it must select the eternal material of art . . . . The higher
processes of art are all processes of simplification."[2]

And again, from her essay "On the Art of Fiction": "Art, it seems to me, should simplify. That, indeed, is very nearly the whole of the higher artistic process; finding what conventions of form and what detail one can do without and yet preserve the spirit of the whole—so that all that one has suppressed and cut away is there to the reader's consciousness as much as if it were in type on the page."[3]

Why stop at Willa Cather, though, if I'm casting back in time for useful models? I might as well go back to *War and Peace*, which we're apt to forget is a novel drawing heavily on research. From this distance, everything in the nineteenth century looks like it happened at the same time, but in fact Tolstoy composed the novel, which starts in 1805 and takes place during the Napoleonic Wars, between 1863 and 1868, or roughly sixty years after the events. He was thirty-five when he began work on it, which, for those of you around that age, is roughly analogous to you writing something set in the mid-twentieth century—during the Second World War, say, or the McCarthy era. While you can't have seen or experienced directly anything from then, you might have living grandparents from whom you could gather stories, as well as friends in their seventies and eighties with vivid memories of those events.

That's roughly the situation in which Tolstoy found himself when he started. In the introduction to their translation of *War and Peace*, Richard Pevear and Larissa Volokhonsky discuss Tolstoy's working method, which is surprisingly recognizable. They describe how, although he first thought that he'd write a novel about an exiled figure returning from Siberia in 1856, after the emperor's pardon, Tolstoy found himself captivated by what he learned about the 1825 uprising that had sent his hero into exile. As he worked his way back to the years of his hero's childhood, he was then drawn into reading about the War of 1812 and—because that, in turn, had its roots in events happening in 1805—he eventually chose to start there. The novel continued to evolve in response to his research, so that he was altering the first parts even as he wrote the later parts. The translators write:

> Coming across a collection of Masonic texts in the library of the Rumyantsev Museum, he became interested and decided to make Pierre Bezukhov a Mason. He studied the people of Moscow at the theaters, in the clubs, in the streets, looking for the types he needed. A great many of his fictional characters, if not all of them, had real-life models. The old Prince Bolkonsky and the old Count Rostov were drawn from Tolstoy's grandfathers, Nikolai Rostov and Princess Marya from his parents, Sonya from one of his aunts. The Rostov estate, Otradnoe, is a reflection of Yasnaya Polyana. Tolstoy spent two days on the battlefield of Borodino and made his own map of the disposition of forces, correcting the maps of the historians. He collected a whole library of materials on the Napoleonic wars, many bits of which also found their way into the fabric of the book. His memory for historical minutiae was prodigious.[4]

Wisely, though, Tolstoy realized that his task was to make history *live*, and that the minutiae on their own weren't important. Rather, it's the way he *translated* what he learned into the wealth of impressions registered by his characters—a horse with a broken leg neighing next to a shattered cannon; Nikolai's startled sense, during the battle in which he's wounded, that the big-nosed Frenchman running at him actually means to harm him; the blood left by one wounded soldier on a cart quickly swabbed away by another soldier to make way for a third to lie down—that makes us feel his characters living in their world. In an essay called "A Few Words Apropos of the Book *War and Peace*," published in 1868 in a Russian journal and included as an appendix to the new translation, Tolstoy writes about "the divergence between my descriptions of historical events and the accounts of historians," which was

not accidental, but inevitable. A historian and an artist, describing a historical epoch, have two completely different objects. As a historian would be wrong if he should try to present a historical figure in all his entirety, in all the complexity of his relations to all sides of life, so an artist would not fulfill his task by always presenting a figure in his historical significance . . .

A historian has to do with the results of an event, the artist with the fact of the event. A historian, describing a battle, says: the left flank of such-and-such army was moved against such-and-such village, cut down the enemy, but was forced to retreat; then the cavalry, going into the attack, overthrew . . . and so on. The historian cannot speak otherwise. And yet these words have no meaning for an artist and do not even touch upon the event itself. The artist, using his own experience, or letters, memoirs, and accounts, derives for himself an image of the event that took place, and quite often (in a battle for example) the conclusion which the historian allows himself to draw about the activity of such-and-such army turns out to be the opposite of the artist's conclusion.[5]

Despite that, though, Tolstoy also notes that

the artist should not forget that the notion of historical figures and events formed among people is based not on fantasy, but on historical documents, insofar as historians have been able to amass them; and therefore, while understanding and present-ing these figures and events differently, the artist ought to be guided, like the historian, by historical materials. *Wherever in my novel historical figures speak and act, I have not invented, but have made use of the materials, of which, during my work, I have formed a whole library.*[6] (Tolstoy's italics)

On the one hand, he says: learn everything, use everything, stick to actions as they're known. On the other hand, he also says: discard all the previous summaries and interpretations of events, discard everything but the living image. Not either/or, but both—which is also what Yourcenar says.

How impossible, you might think. Tolstoy was a genius, Yourcenar too—what can I learn from them? You can learn a lot; you can learn how to do this well. For all the examples of bad fic-tion based on too much research poorly employed, there are also many beautiful examples in which writers have done just what Tolstoy did, learning whatever it was they wanted to learn until it became known to them as they know their own pasts, and then *embodying* that knowledge in character and action, rather than just plopping it onto the page.

Just to mention a few: think of Pat Barker's wonderful *Regeneration* trilogy about World War I, or any Penelope Fitzgerald or David Malouf novel. Think of William Kennedy's *Ironweed*, or Edward P. Jones's *The Known World*; Marilynne Robinson's *Gilead*, or Margot Livesey's *Eva Moves the Furniture*. The transformation works in stories, too: look at Allan Gurganus's "Reassurance," which breathes life into Walt Whitman's work as a nurse in a military hospital, or Ray Carver's final story, "Errand," which brings us Chekhov's last days. Many of Jim Shepard's stories brilliantly illuminate historical figures, as do such Angela Carter stories as "Our Lady of the Massacre." Think of Ron Hansen's "Wickedness," which turns on the experiences of people caught in the blizzard of 1888, and of Alistair MacLeod's beautiful story "As Birds Bring Forth the Sun," which, in a few pages, conveys the feel of two centuries in the lives of Scottish immigrants to Nova Scotia. The stories Alice Munro collected in *Open Secrets* offer a master class in how to use research in fiction; so too does William Trevor's "The News from Ireland," which reimagines the great Irish famine of the 1840s. His characters take on such absolute life that we may not be aware at first that they also exemplify certain social classes and attitudes, catching a whole time and place in a handful of individuals.

In her story "Meneseteung," Munro created a protagonist, Almeda Roth, who may be an "actual" person; the unnamed narrator uses documentary evidence to suggest that she is. But because the setting is a small Canadian town unfamiliar to many readers, and the protagonist unsung if not unknown, we can't know whether Almeda is "real" without retracing Munro's footsteps. The point is the deep reimagining of Almeda's life, which also illuminates a set of social attitudes and a moment in Canadian history as no work of social science ever could. In the last section, Munro jolts us back to her documenting first-person narrator, summarizing the last years of Almeda's life and then closing the story like this:

> I thought that there wasn't anybody alive in the world but me who would know this, who would make the connection. And I would be the last person to do so. But perhaps this isn't so. People are curious. A few people are. They will be driven to find things out, even trivial things. They will put things together. You see them going around with notebooks, scraping the dirt off gravestones, reading microfilm, just in the hope of seeing this trickle in time, making a connection, rescuing one thing from the rubbish.[7]

Isn't that what we're about with all our writing? The old advice to "write what you know" is true in one way, but not in the most limited way: it doesn't mean we can only write about what we know directly from our own experiences. A more generous, more useful interpretation of the phrase is that we should write about what we know, *however we come to know it*, whether by vision or sensual experience or reading or conversation or passionate imagining. That, in the end, is what the research is for.

NOTES

1. Yourcenar, Marguerite, *Memoirs of Hadrian: Followed by Reflections on the Composition of Memoirs of Hadrian*. Translated by Grace Frick, in collaboration with the author. (New York: The Noonday Press, 1990), 329–30.

2. Cather, Willa, *Stories, Poems, and Other Writings* (New York: The Library of America, 1992), 836.

3. Ibid., 939.

4. Richard Pevear and Larissa Volokhonsky, introduction to *War and Peace*, by Leo Tolstoy. Translated by Richard Pevear and Larissa Volokhonsky. (New York: Alfred A. Knopf, 2007), ix.

5. Richard Pevear and Larissa Volokhonsky, appendix to *War and Peace*, by Leo Tolstoy. (New York: Alfred A. Knopf, 2007), 1219–20.

6. Ibid., 1222.

7. Munro, Alice, "Meneseteung," in *Friend of My Youth* (New York: Vintage Contemporaries, 1991), 73.

THE SWORD OF DAMOCLES:

On Suspense, Shower Murders, and Shooting People on the Beach

ANTHONY DOERR

1. Beach Scene

TRAVEL WITH ME to French Algiers, just before the Second World War, where Meursault is an alienated, anomalous fellow who, upon learning his mother has died, does none of the typical sobbing or hair tearing or weepy paging through scrapbooks a reader might be accustomed to seeing upon reading of the deaths of protagonists' mothers.

Instead, during the days following her death, Meursault helps his neighbor, a very sketchy customer named Raymond, who may or may not be a pimp, take revenge on his girlfriend, who may or may not be cheating on Raymond. To be specific, Raymond asks Meursault to write a breakup letter for him, "a real stinker, that'll get her on the raw." Meursault does. A couple of days later, Raymond and Meursault run into the girl's brother and a friend on the beach. These two are Arabs.

There's a knife fight. Raymond is wounded. Meursault takes
a pistol from Raymond so that he won't do anything too crazy.
Then Meursault heads back out onto the beach:

As I slowly walked toward the boulders at the end of the beach
I could feel my temples swelling under the impact of the light. It
pressed itself on me, trying to check my progress. And each time
I felt a hot blast strike my forehead, I gritted my teeth, I clenched
my fists in my trouser pockets and keyed up every nerve to fend
off the sun and the dark befuddlement it was pouring into me.
Whenever a blade of vivid light shot upward from a bit of shell or
broken glass lying on the sand, my jaws set hard. I wasn't going
to be beaten, and I walked steadily on.

The small black hump of rock came into view far down the
beach. It was rimmed by a dazzling sheen of light and feathery
spray, but I was thinking of the cold, clear stream behind it, and
longing to hear again the tinkle of running water. Anything to
be rid of the glare, the sight of women in tears, the strain and
effort—and to retrieve the pool of shadow by the rock and its
cool silence!

But when I came nearer I saw that Raymond's Arab had
returned. He was by himself this time, lying on his back, his
hands behind his head, his face shaded by the rock while the sun
beat on the rest of his body. One could see his dungarees steam-
ing in the heat. I was rather taken aback; my impression had
been that the incident was closed, and I hadn't given a thought
to it on my way here.

On seeing me, the Arab raised himself a little, and his hand
went to his pocket. Naturally, I gripped Raymond's revolver in

the pocket of my coat. Then the Arab let himself sink back again, but without taking his hand from his pocket. I was some distance off, at least ten yards, and most of the time I saw him as a blurred dark form wobbling in the heat haze. Sometimes, however, I had glimpses of his eyes glowing between the half-closed lids. The sound of the waves was even lazier, feebler, than at noon. But the light hadn't changed; it was pounding as fiercely as ever on the long stretch of sand that ended at the rock. For two hours the sun seemed to have made no progress; becalmed in a sea of molten steel. Far out on the horizon a steamer was passing; I could just make out from the corner of an eye the small black moving patch, while I kept my gaze fixed on the Arab.

It struck me that all I had to do was to turn, walk away, and think no more about it. But the whole beach, pulsing with heat, was pressing on my back. I took some steps toward the stream. The Arab didn't move. After all, there was still some distance between us. Perhaps because of the shadow on his face, he seemed to be grinning at me.

I waited. The heat was beginning to scorch my cheeks; beads of sweat were gathering in my eyebrows. It was just the same sort of heat as at my mother's funeral, and I had the same dis-agreeable sensations—especially in my forehead, where all the veins seemed to be bursting through the skin. I couldn't stand it any longer, and took another step forward. I knew it was a fool thing to do; I wouldn't get out of the sun by moving on a yard or so. But I took that step, just one step, forward. And then the Arab drew his knife and held it up toward me, athwart the sunlight.

A shaft of light shot upward from the steel, and I felt as if a long, thin blade transfixed my forehead. At the same moment all the sweat that had accumulated in my eyebrows splashed down on my eyelids, covering them with a warm film of moisture. Beneath a veil of brine and tears my eyes were blinded; I was conscious only of the cymbals of the sun clashing on my skull, and, less distinctly, of the keen blade of light flashing up from the knife, scarring my eyelashes, and gouging into my eyeballs.

Then everything began to reel before my eyes, a fiery gust came from the sea, while the sky cracked in two, from end to end, and a great sheet of flame poured down through the rift. Every nerve in my body was a steel spring, and my grip closed on the revolver. The trigger gave, and the smooth underbelly of the butt jogged my palm. And so, with that crisp, whipcrack sound, it all began. I shook off my sweat and the clinging veil of light. I knew I'd shattered the balance of the day, the spacious calm of this beach on which I had been happy. But I fired four shots more into the inert body, on which they left no visible trace. And each successive shot was another loud, fateful rap on the door of my undoing.

2. Two Disclaimers

ONE: I'M AN absolutely terrible writer of suspense. I use up most of my sentences describing trees or snow or light. I also tend to think it's interesting to spend sentences on esoteric subjects such as the types of bombs dropped on Hamburg in 1945 or what happens to the blood of wood frogs in winter. (It crystallizes. When you drop a frozen, still-living wood frog onto the floor of a lab, it will make a clinking sound.) It is safe to say, actually, that I am possibly the worst suspense writer in America.

TWO: Though often I prove willing to pay ten dollars to watch films that are deemed "suspenseful," only to inevitably feel dirty afterward, nine times out of ten, I'm not interested in the kind of suspense that becomes melodrama—Kurt Russell, James Bond, Keanu Reeves, car-chase-style suspense in which the action is so profoundly stressed that it blots out everything else, including plausibility, character, physical detail, humor, and the higher registers of one's hearing.

I'm more interested in measured, proportionally handled suspense; the kind of suspense that makes you simultaneously want to skip forward a few paragraphs to find out what will happen and dwell for as long as possible inside the slow blister of rising action. I'm interested in the moment in space and time when the narrative is reduced to a state of suspension at the apex of its ascent, seemingly delayed a millisecond at the very top of the inverted parabola, flooded with light, just before it begins its fall.

Indeed, even if the phrase is a redundant oxymoron, I'm most interested in suspended suspense.

3. Definition

SUSPENSE IS, LITERALLY, the temporary cessation of something. As in, you're suspended from school; your sentence is suspended; you're suspended in a solution; you're suspended in midair. Its origin comes from the Latin *suspendere*, and inside of *suspendere* is the word *pendere*, which means "to hang."

When we say a misfortune is "im-pend-ing," we mean that it is "hanging" over us. Someone who is "de-pend-ent" on his friends is "hanging on" them; without their support, he falls to the ground. To "ap-pend" an "ap-pend-age" or an "ap-pend-ix" onto something is to "cause to hang something." "Sus-pend-ers" hold up your pants, and a "pend-ant" hangs from your neck.

And someone who is in "sus-pense" is literally hanging. She is in abeyance, she is on tenterhooks; she is, as the *Online Etymology Dictionary* puts it, "not rendered, not paid, not carried out."

4. Arnold Friend and the Screen Door

IN ALMOST EVERY suspenseful moment in the history of drama, a hero (and therefore also a reader) finds herself caught between two points and dangles there a while, on the threshold between two worlds, *suspended,* before crossing over to one of two poles.

Suspense happens in the pause, the drawing out, the tense, vibrating position as our hero hovers above the abyss, before the large-scale dramatic questions get answered—Will she fall? Will she cross to safety?—a place where the hero (and therefore the reader) feels both the intoxication of gravity and the terror of it, before these emotions are resolved. These moments are at the heart of storytelling.

The author Steve Almond is fond of telling his students that a reader comes into a story with two questions: Who do I care about? and What does he or she care about? I want to add that as a reader enters a narrative, it in turn begins to pose to her a sequence of dramatic questions. In the case of, say, Joseph

Conrad's *Heart of Darkness*, those questions might be along these lines: Where is this Kurtz, anyway? Will Marlow survive this attack by the "natives"? Will Kurtz be as grandiose as Marlow expects? And these smaller dramatic questions form a foundation upon which stand larger dramatic questions, such as Will Marlow succeed? Why is he telling this story? Is restraint really what makes civilized people civilized? This builds until the reader rises to the top, the capstone, the largest dramatic questions, the ones that are supported by all the little, more quotidian questions stratified beneath them. With *Heart of Darkness*, those big questions might be simplified into something like Is imperialism an abomination?

Here's a snapshot from Joyce Carol Oates's "Where Are You Going, Where Have You Been?":

She rushed forward and tried to lock the door. Her fingers were shaking. "But why lock it," Arnold Friend said gently, talking right into her face. "It's just a screen door. It's just nothing . . . I mean, anybody can break through a screen door and glass and wood and iron or anything else if he needs to, anybody at all, and specially Arnold Friend. If the place got lit up with a fire, honey, you'd come runnin' out into my arms, right into my arms an' safe at home—like you knew I was your lover and'd stopped fooling around. I don't mind a nice shy girl but I don't like no fooling around."

. . . Connie stood barefoot on the linoleum floor, staring at him. "What do you want?" she whispered.

"I want you," he said.

Even if you don't know this story, you can apprehend from this scene its fundamental dramatic question: Will Connie stay in the house or will she go out to Arnold's car? Upon which stands the next layer of questions: Is Arnold the devil? Will Connie keep her innocence? The fulcrum here is in a literal sense the screen door, and Connie is dangling on its threshold, with two drastically different worlds on either side: safety and innocence in the house of her childhood; and danger and experience purring out in the driveway in Arnold Friend's car. Arnold Friend wants Connie and Connie wants *something*—she wants to shed her innocence; she wants to live. The question is whether Connie also wants to die, and if Arnold Friend is an obstacle inhibiting her from achieving what she wants or a vehicle to deliver her to the object of her longing.

The title echoes what might be considered the largest dramatic questions: Where are you going, reader? and Where have you been? Connie and the reader find themselves together on a threshold, behind which is every place they have been and ahead of which is every place they might go. The bright solidity of Connie's youthful identity will either be barely, at the last moment, preserved, or it will be forced out, obliterated, and also possibly opened up by the demonic and relentless Arnold Friend. Any reader who has lived past the age of fourteen has probably stood on some version of this same threshold.

The screen door, which Arnold Friend says "is just a screen door. It's just nothing" is the high wire upon which Connie wobbles; it is the river in *Heart of Darkness*, the road in *The Road*, the beach in *The Stranger*, the sea in *Moby-Dick*, home in *The Odyssey*.

5. Minnie Mouse Tied to the Train Tracks While Mickey Mouse Rushes to Save Her

IN ALL STORYTELLING, no matter how nonlinear or diffuse the narrative might be, no matter how whimsical the pacing is, some kind of time bomb should always be ticking toward zero. There's always—even in a Lydia Davis story, or a Ben Marcus story, or a Gary Lutz story, or an Amy Hempel story—*pressure*. There might not literally be a cavalry sweeping across the meadow just as a gun is put to a hostage's head, but all storytelling demands some level of pressure. Maybe it comes from the fading daylight, or the bad guys assembling a car bomb in their hideout, or the disintegrating marriage, or the encroaching storm, or from tensions within the language of the story itself. In almost every story of any merit there is a "beach, pulsing with heat," pressing on the protagonist's back, or a screen door behind which the protagonist wobbles. Someone is tied to the train tracks and the train is approaching and the literal or figurative hero, who has been chained to the reader by now, is beset by obstacles on his or her way to rescue that someone, and in archetypal drama the question of whether the hero will make it in time is both always in doubt and never in doubt.

My argument here is that we want our heroes to take a painfully, ecstatically, drastically long time to get there.

6. David Mamet's Perfect Sports Argument

AN ELEMENTARY, BUT hopefully useful way to look at narrative structure is to look at sports. Sports are both highly popular and highly shaped. Sports are built upon the foundations of dramatic storytelling, and we've been refining their structures—both simplifying them by trimming out old rules and complicating them by adding new ones—for thousands of years.

For a writer's purposes, consider that for the next few paragraphs, superstars are protagonists, and fans are readers. In terms of dramatics, when you have a favorite team or a favorite player, it or he or she becomes your hero. Your favorite player wants to win, and you want what she wants. Longing is the fundamental emotion here, and story arises from the obstacles that rear up between the hero and the object of her longing, which in sports is usually embodied in a big, gleaming, thirty-pound golden talisman named for somebody who is dead. One way to look at games, tournaments, and seasons is that they are essentially highly formalized structures designed to produce obstacles. Why? Because obstacles produce delay, and delay produces compelling narrative.

Let's say it's a Saturday evening, it's the play-offs, your kids are somewhere else, you've got the pregame on, and your absolutely favorite team is about to take the field/court/ice/whatever. You watch the players run their drills, you listen to the prognosticators recite their ridiculous keys to the game, and then you ask yourself: What does the perfect game look like? In David Mamet's *Three Uses of the Knife: On the Nature and Purpose of Drama*, he puts it like this: "Do we wish for Our Team to take the field and thrash the opposition from the First Moment?" We might think we do, but, truly, when I'm in this situation, and I've got a fistful of fluorescent orange chips halfway to my mouth, I'm hoping for something more dramatic. I'm hoping for a great game, a test, a classic, an ordeal. Again, here's Mamet:

"We wish for a closely fought match that contains many satisfying reversals, but which can be seen, retroactively, to have always tended toward a satisfying and inevitable conclusion."

So, briefly, in a three-act structure, with cues stolen from Mamet, here is my perfect game. In act 1, my favorite team takes the court/ice/field/whatever and plays well. The first five minutes look good: the offense is clicking, the defense has made a stop, the referees are "letting them play," as they say, and soon my favorite team has the ball again and the players are driving and it looks like they are about to take a fairly significant lead.

Suddenly, there's an error, a mistake, a fumble. The opposing team pushes forward with, in Mamet's words, "previously unsuspected strength and imagination." This is unexpected. In dramatics, this is called "the ordeal."

Now it's act 2, and my favorite team starts screwing up badly—missed blocks, moving picks, mishandling a clean throw to first base, false starts, et cetera. Clearly, it, too, has underestimated the opponent.

Then even my favorite player screws up. He or she throws an interception for a touchdown, fumbles, strikes out, drops a fairly easy catch, or misses an easy dunk. My favorite team is sinking into the trough of despondency—heads hang, coach calls a time-out, someone throws a racket, someone isn't listening during the huddle.

And now things are becoming almost ridiculously stacked against my hopes: the opposing team has become more than just an opposing team; it's an enemy, a true antagonist. The antagonist is canny and shrewd and my belief in my favorite team's ability to win is terribly, perhaps irrevocably, shaken. Of course, now is the time to remind the fans (your readers) that the clock is running down relentlessly. All seems irredeemably lost. Act 2 ends.

But, thank the Lord (sometimes literally, in dramatics), in act 3, help arrives from an unexpected corner, maybe from a bench player: someone makes a block, or an umpire calls somebody safe, or a defensive lineman makes an interception, or the third-string point guard makes a three-pointer, and suddenly the gap in the score begins to close. There is a glimmer of possibility, and now your favorite team is roused, you're standing on the sofa, you've crushed several Doritos into the carpet, your team is standing up straight again, the body language is good, the crowd is waving ridiculous yellow towels as if summoning angels from heaven, as if calling down the very power of the gods.

And soon—miraculously—your team has managed to tie the game.

All this time, the clock is winding down. Pressure is being applied. But don't worry, the moral lessons of the second act are not lost on your favorite team, and here comes the language of mythic structure: they have LEARNED, they have COME OF AGE, they have been BAPTIZED and are REBORN, and though there probably isn't enough time left to pull off a victory, there just might be, if the hero delivers what you know she can at this exact moment, and the team rouses itself for one last effort, one last push toward the impossible, the Hail Mary . . .

It has come down to the final moment, the catch-and-shoot, the forty-foot putt, the shotgun snap, the prayer. It comes down to the lone hero in whom so much hope and feeling has been invested. Will he prevail? Will the hero attain what she has longed for all her career? Will you, the reader, the fan, the vicarious onlooker, get what you have longed for since you began this particular journey? The dramatic questions are finally going to be answered. And you want them to be answered. You're desperate for them to be answered. But, first, you are suspended at this most critical moment.

Because now there's a commercial break in which a man with a foam sphere for a head tries to sell you a Jumbo Jack Hamburger with two tacos on the side.

7. Why?

ACCORDING TO A report by the Nielsen company, the average American watches 153 hours of television per month, and a huge percentage of that television is highly structured narrative, that is, sports, drama, situation comedies, game shows, or reality TV.

Why? Why do we crave so much story?

Perhaps it's because drama offers us an exercise in vicariousness. Story is a form of play. Writing and reading, too, are forms of play. And play is our way of practicing life and death. In *The Art Instinct*, the critic Denis Dutton proposes that the arts are "evolutionary adaptations," that our interest in stories is programmed into our very cells by evolution. Maybe there is an evolutionary advantage in any species that can pass information to one another through stories.

Don't eat that flower, one of our ancestors tells another, because it made my grandmother sick for a week.

Don't go down to the creek, one of our ancestors tells a passing family of strangers. Last year there were crocodiles down there.

In Dutton's line of thought, stories are a way of using past events to model future ones. The critic Laura Miller puts it like this: story, she says, is "the enjoyable means by which we practice and hone certain abilities likely to come in handy in more serious situations."

Drama, from Mother Goose to *Shrek* to *The Stranger* to *War and Peace*, offers us anxiety, but it is anxiety experienced in the safety of an armchair. If our favorite basketball player misses that three-pointer at the buzzer, we feel disappointed, sure, and if we're very young and the experience is new to us, we might even feel anguish. But we know all the while we're safe on our Empire-style Pottery Barn sofa with tapered legs and kiln-dried wood, built by mothers in Thailand whose lives we work very hard not to imagine.

If the horror-movie boyfriend of the tank top–wearing heroine has just told her, "Let's split up. I'll look in the attic, you check the basement," and she's walking down the stairs where it is SO OBVIOUS that the freaky disfigured mask-wearing killer is looming with a six-foot scimitar, we watch because we know the anxiety we feel is not quite real. We know we are safe in our theater seats.

But eventually, in the simplest stories, all the little quotidian dramatic questions get answered; our team wins or loses, the heroine gets eviscerated or decapitates the killer with a screwdriver, and we roll up the Doritos bag and turn on the lights and confront the much larger, much less structured, and much more real anxieties of our lives.

We weep for characters, and then we go brush our teeth and have to face the fact that the world is warming at such a rapid pace that a terrifying number of amphibians are vanishing every month. And so through plays, through soccer games, through novels, through movies, through video games, through political elections—through story—we rehearse feelings we might eventually need in our own lives.

Because, fundamentally, story promises to order the unorderable, to impress a system on the unsystematic. Story promises to impose a meaningful structure on a universe that resists meaning and structure.

Through drama, in the moments of greatest suspense, when the hero is hanging by a support from above, swaying to and fro, when the future remains in shadow, we rehearse anxiety and longing more profoundly than any other emotions. Anxiety is the terror that our hero (and therefore, vicariously, we) will fail, that the obstacles will overcome him. The hero will plunge into the abyss, drown, be eaten, lose the love interest, et cetera.

And longing is the reach, the extension, the wild desire to attain the next stable platform at the end of the high wire. It's the hope against hope that the water shooting out of the fountain will stay aloft forever.

8. Anxiety #1

HERE'S A FRACTION of a scene from Cormac McCarthy's *The Road*, in which a father and son wake to discover a phalanx of cannibals (yes, cannibals) marching toward them:

> An army in tennis shoes, tramping. Carrying three-foot lengths of pipe with leather wrappings. Lanyards at the wrist.

Some of the pipes were threaded through with lengths of chain fitted at their ends with every manner of bludgeon. They clanked past, marching with a swaying gait like wind-up toys. Bearded, their breath smoking through their masks. Shh, he said. Shh. The phalanx following carried spears or lances tassled with ribbons, the long blades hammered out of trucksprings in some crude forge upcountry. The boy lay with his face in his arms, terrified. They passed two hundred feet away, the ground shuddering lightly. Tramping. Behind them came wagons drawn by slaves in harness and piled with goods of war and after that the women, perhaps a dozen in number, some of them pregnant, and lastly a supplementary consort of catamites illclothed against the cold and fitted in dogcollars and yoked each to each.

McCarthy repeats words ("tramping," "pipe") to slow down the action; he alternates glances back and forth from heroes to danger, heroes to danger. The reader watches the awful crew in much the way the boy might, if he could bear to look: mesmerized, horrified, and with excruciating detail. Father and son have been surprised, they are in the moral right, they are hopelessly outnumbered; all these are very common techniques used to build suspense. In the ensuing sentences McCarthy even goes so far as to have the son call the horrific gang passing on the road the "bad guys."

The two necessary poles have been drawn: protagonist and antagonist, favorite team and opposing team. Our heroes are placed on a threshold between peril and safety, and because things are drawn so clearly, as they are in most Westerns, the reader feels the characters' anxiety quite acutely: the fear of death, the fear of being enslaved, the fear of being eaten. And we get a sense of modulation in this anxiety: by the end of the scene we know the bad guys have "passed on," but we also believe that we have not finished seeing bad guys. We have plenty of pages left to read, and the relative safety in which the man and boy find themselves— that is, the provisional resolution—is temporary and fragile.

One baseline dramatic question—Are they going to be spotted right now by the horrific bad guys with the slaves?—has been answered. But a larger dramatic question—What the heck is going to happen to this little boy?—is not yet answered. And so we keep reading.

9. Anxiety #2

IN EDGAR ALLAN Poe's "The Tell-Tale Heart," our point of view is rooted on the other side; we watch from the POV of the bad guy. In the following quote, the murderer, carrying a veiled lantern with a single dim ray escaping it, stands in an old man's room, preparing to murder him in his bed. The light has fallen upon the open eye of the old man:

> But even yet I refrained and kept still. I scarcely breathed. I held the lantern motionless. I tried how steadily I could maintain the ray upon the eye. Meantime the hellish tattoo of the heart increased. It grew quicker and quicker, and louder and louder every instant. The old man's terror *must* have been extreme! It grew louder, I say, louder every moment!—do you mark me well? I have told you that I am nervous: so I am. And now at

the dead hour of the night, amid the dreadful silence of that old house, so strange a noise as this excited me to uncontrollable terror. Yet, for some minutes longer I refrained and stood still. But the beating grew louder, louder! I thought the heart must burst. And now a new anxiety seized me—the sound would be heard by a neighbour! The old man's hour had come!

In this case, we feel anxiety for both murderer and victim. Again we see, even in this snippet of scene, the reversals, Poe's musical technique of delay, the *slowing* down and pausing. We see that a large percentage of this entire paragraph is devoted not to accelerating the action, but to *impeding* it.

10. Science

BOTH MCCARTHY AND Poe take their time. McCarthy takes his time letting the bad guys troll slowly across the road. Poe strands his madman in the darkness at the foot of his victim's bed for what seems like hours. ("Yet, for some minutes longer I refrained and stood still.") Indeed, maybe the entirety of Poe's story, really, consists of delay.

Perhaps these pauses, so long as they don't last too long, this *suspending* of the character and the reader over the abyss, this *hanging*, are so often used in successful storytelling because there is something cooked into human beings that craves it. We like breaks between sets during rock concerts, intermissions during plays; we like to space our cigarettes throughout the day; we like to feast during Carnival, and get drunk on Mardi Gras, and then have forty days of self-denial before getting drunk again on Easter. We sip our scotch (some of us) rather than chug it. We urge our kids to open their biggest Christmas presents last. We like to get out of the hot tub halfway through a soak and roll in the snow before getting back in. We like cliff-hangers in serialized fiction. We want our games to go into overtime; we save our favorite chocolates for last.

Indeed, a couple of studies published in 2008 and 2009 found that disruptions sometimes enhance our enjoyment of pleasurable activities. An experiment at New York University found that students who watched a sitcom with commercial interruptions experienced more pleasure than those who watched the same show without commercials. Another found that people who had massages interrupted and then resumed reported a higher degree of pleasure than folks who had uninterrupted massages.

This brings us to the law of diminishing returns, an old economic generalization, which basically says that beyond a certain production level, productivity increases at a decreasing rate.

Look at it this way: You've got a garden and you grow tomatoes and one year you grow one hundred tomatoes. The next year, you do everything the same, except you add one pound of fertilizer and you get two hundred tomatoes. But if you were to add two pounds of fertilizer, you wouldn't get three hundred tomatoes; you might get two hundred and fifty. Applying three pounds of fertilizer may still increase the harvest, but perhaps by only a very little bit. And applying four pounds of fertilizer turns out to be a very bad move: you start burning the roots. Add five pounds and you might get no tomatoes at all.

In terms of a storyteller's purposes, the argument goes like this: according to the law of diminishing returns, the first bite of chocolate, the first drag of a cigarette, the first lick of ice cream, the first intoxicating moments of climactic action in a novel are the most powerful moments because they are relatively and recently new to us. Then, because of the law of diminishing returns, we quickly get habituated to them. We crave newness, but we habituate quickly to things, whether it's discomfort or travel or bites of chocolate or marriage.

Maybe interruptions—slowing down scenes just at their most pleasurable—are a way of making the sensations of vicarious anxiety and longing feel acute to us for as long as possible.

11. Back to the Beach

IT'S OFTEN ASSUMED by beginning writers that suspenseful scenes need to be quickly paced. But something I find over and over in drafts of my students' fiction, and in drafts of my own, is that we tend to rush through the scenes we want to be most suspenseful. I've seen a student spend eight sentences putting characters in a van only to spend two sentence fragments sending the van across the ice and into an intersection.

Common sense says that slow scenes should move slowly and fast scenes should move quickly. Quick cuts, sharp angles, hurry up and rush to the space break. I do this all the time: climactic scenes are hard to write, and when I finally make myself write them, I find myself sprinting through the dialogue, skimping on the physical detail, and rushing the characters into their conflict. I'm forever dying to hit return a couple of times and start in on the aftermath.

But the best advice is probably just the opposite: a huge percentage of writing your most climactic, emotional scenes is about learning to go very slowly. One has to learn to trawl the attention through the texture of the dream.

Let's go back to the Algerian beach with Meursault. How many of these sentences of Camus's are devoted entirely to suspending Meursault above the abyss? How many of Camus's sentences serve the purpose of interrupting, delaying, and prolonging the action? If we eliminate everything except the clearly active sentences, the sentences in which Meursault actually does something and advances the plot of *The Stranger*, the excerpt reads very differently:

As I slowly walked toward the boulders at the end of the beach I could feel my temples swelling under the impact of the light. . . . I walked steadily on.

The small black hump of rock came into view far down the beach. . . . When I came nearer I saw that Raymond's Arab had returned. He was by himself this time, lying on his back, his hands behind his head, his face shaded by the rock while the sun beat on the rest of his body. . . .

On seeing me, the Arab raised himself a little, and his hand went to his pocket. Naturally, I gripped Raymond's revolver in the pocket of my coat. Then the Arab let himself sink back again, but without taking his hand from his pocket. I was some distance off, at least ten yards. . . . I took some steps toward the stream. The Arab didn't move. . . . I couldn't stand it any longer, and took another step forward. . . . And then the Arab drew his knife and held it up toward me, athwart the sunlight.

. . . . My grip closed on the revolver. The trigger gave, and the smooth underbelly of the butt jogged my palm. And so, with that crisp, whipcrack sound, it all began. . . . I fired four shots more into the inert body, on which they left no visible trace.

It's awfully important for a student writer to notice that if you trim out the sentences that serve mostly to interrupt, delay, and prolong the reader's anxiety, hardly anything remains. The pace is quicker, the information is still delivered to the reader, but the intensity is gone. If you eliminate all of Camus's careful work to extend his reader's vicarious anxiety, Meursault doesn't hover above the abyss, suspended for a blinding, overheated, faux eternity; he simply falls into it.

12. Information

A LARGE PART of storytelling has to do with something many creative writing teachers call "the rate of revelation." How quickly do you want to unspool your secrets? How quickly do you want to answer the dramatic questions you've posed? How quickly do you want to let your reader know everything that you (the story-teller) know? The most common thing I see beginning writers do, second perhaps only to rushing through their most emotionally important scenes, is withhold crucial information from their readers. For some mystifying reason, many student writers think it's intriguing to keep information from a reader. Several times a year, I read a draft of a story that withholds a whole bunch of information until the very end, then dumps it all over the reader in one wallop in the last paragraph.

It is intriguing sometimes to withhold information from one of your *characters*. This is a very common ploy in classic Hitchockian suspense; Hitchcock is a master at showing the audience what the characters don't see. In *Family Plot*, he shows the audience that brake fluid is leaking out of a car before the characters pile into it to head down a twisty mountain road. The viewer knows about the crazy mother in *Psycho* before the detective (actor Martin Balsam) does, making the scene in which Balsam enters the house one of the most famous scenes in cinema. In these scenes, Hitchcock is withholding information from certain characters, but he is absolutely feeding it to his viewers.

I'd argue that in almost every case, a storyteller should give her readers as much information as possible as soon as possible. If a piano will drop on your character's head in paragraph eight, show it dangling from a rope in paragraph one. If the grocery store where your character works is about to be robbed, show the burglar out in the parking lot pulling the panty hose over his head. These are perhaps obvious pieces of advice but they work: show the train coming down the tracks, the gun under the cushion, the husband's footsteps coming up the front walk as his wife climbs on top of the gardener in the backyard. In Joseph Conrad's novel *The Secret Agent*, things are so much more interesting once you know the little man called "the Professor" has dynamite wired to his body. If a character has a secret and all of his or her behavior is in some slight way steered by that secret, it is not suspenseful to conceal that secret from your reader. It's unfair. The reader is left out of the conversation, and rather than feel excited, he or she will feel excluded, and soon after that: bored.

A reader should have as complete an understanding of what's going on in a scene as possible. Information is the river in story-telling and the reader always needs clean, fresh information flowing past.

13. Longing Is Like the Seed

ONE FINAL REITERATION, for you and for me. Take your time. Don't take forever, but take your time. Interruptions, as I've tried to argue, can build intensity, rather than sap it.

I'm not suggesting that interruptions need to be as disruptive as a stranger walking in on you while you're having a massage. You don't have to wake your reader from the dream. But I do believe that a reader wants to savor the anxiety you've generated in your work before you let her overcome it. If she's like most humans, she wants to hear Arnold Friend talk; she wants to feel the Algerian heat beginning to scorch her cheeks; she wants to see the terrible bad guys "clank past, marching with a swaying gait like wind-up toys." Because as soon as that one installment is complete, as soon as "victory" is proclaimed, as soon as the vehicle reaches the top of the ramp, as soon as that particular dramatic question is resolved (Will Connie stay behind the screen door? Will Meursault pull the trigger? Will the boy and his father get captured?), then the real anxiety of the world, its great baffling, unsystematic disorder, reasserts itself.

And then she'll have to turn to another story, another vicarious rehearsal of anxiety and longing, another partner. We go from our televisions to our books, from our computers to our telephones, from stories told over dinner to the movie theater across the street. We crave stories because they give us some sense that life can be structured and resolved, and yet we don't want our resolutions too soon, because as soon as we get them, we're going to need to go elsewhere and pinion ourselves against a new set of vicarious life-or-death emotions.

Here's an Emily Dickinson poem that says all this and more, and far better than I can:

> Longing is like the Seed
> That wrestles in the Ground,
> Believing if it intercede
> It shall at length be found.
>
> The Hour, and the Clime,
> Each Circumstance unknown—
> What Constancy must be achieved
> Before it see the Sun!

Suspense, for me, is the constancy rather than the car chase, it's the *at length*, the hour unknown, the clime unknown. It's winter now, but spring is coming eventually—it has to come, you have to believe it's coming. For now you hover, you wrestle in the ground, you rehearse your life through someone else's, and through repetition of the act of vicariousness, you develop empathy: you come to believe that another person has feelings and desires and intentions, you come to believe you are not alone in the world, that through books you can have deep, significant conversations with other consciousnesses.

We read because of the chance that tomorrow we might choose a book from a shelf, open it, and feel a connection that transcends the barriers of generations and continents and lets us stare into the soul of someone we've never met, and maybe never *could* meet. Through story, we humans make attempts, several times a day, to connect with one another. Through story, we convince ourselves that our experiences of the world are not nearly as different as they appear.

"A SORT OF LEANING AGAINST":
Writing With, From, and For Others

MAGGIE NELSON

FOR A LONG time, I worried there was something wrong with me as a writer, because I leaned so heavily against the thinking and writing of others. And further, that instead of wanting to hide that leaning, my impulse has often been to showcase it, to make this thinking-with-others, this weaving of mine and others' words, part of the texture of my writing.

The flip side of this "leaning against" has been well put by Emerson, that sage of self-reliance, who famously said: "I hate quotations. Tell me what you know." This is also good advice. "Leaning against" can't be an excuse that saves one from doing the real thinking and writing. I still struggle with this balance. I'm not saying I always get it right. What I'm saying is that it can be a worthwhile and generative place in which to experiment, stumble around, live, and create.

The phrase "a sort of leaning against" comes from Alice Notley's poem "Lady Poverty." Here's the passage in full:

Beginning in poverty as a baby there is nothing
for one but another's food and warmth
should there ever be more
than a sort of leaning against and trust a food for
another from out of one—that would be
poverty—we're taught not to count on
anyone, to be rich,
youthful, empowered
but now I seem to know that the name of a self is poverty
that the pronoun I means such and that starting so
poorly, I can live

"The name of a self is poverty"—I like this. It's a good place
to start, especially for those of us who are born creators, but who
feel annoyed or excluded from the notion of a writer as someone
who has a highly "active imagination" or one who creates "great
images."

I don't really think I have much of an imagination at all, at least
not in the traditional sense of making stuff up or feeling compelled
by things that aren't there. Whatever imagination I have, I think
it's a formal one: I have an intuition for form, for how form and
content depend upon each other. I also have a strong sense of how
ideas are things, things that can be arranged, synthesized, associ-
ated, and *felt*, à la Keats's great phrase "Axioms are not axioms
until they are proved upon our pulses." In my mind, I don't hear
characters talking; I see book shapes; I hear tonal juxtapositions;
I hear music shepherded around the page; I imagine what kind of
sentence or shape could or should house a particular idea.

For many years, I had a quote by the Chinese poet Mo Fei on my wall; it reads: "Poetry has to do with a satisfaction with limited things, a paring down. It is the acceptance of a certain form of poverty. It is not endless construction." This sense of surrender resonated with me. It helped me with my writing (and living) far more than enthusiastic encouragements to just go for it, to let loose one's rampant creativity. Likely, it resonates a bit more for those of us entranced by the generative limitations of nonfiction writing, which Janet Malcolm once usefully compared to renting rather than owning—in which case the writer/renter "must abide by the conditions of his Lease, which stipulates that he leave the house—and its name is Actuality—as he found it."

You might notice that in "Lady Poverty," Notley venerates this "leaning against" as a kind of ethic; so does Mo Fei. Actually, in both cases, the veneration of a certain kind of poverty is more than an ethic—it's almost a theological, or at least spiritual, conviction, devotion, or practice. I'm not going to argue that this "leaning against," in art or in life, is a more advanced or useful ethical, spiritual, or political posture. I'm wary of people venerating what they happen to tend toward, personally, as the better route to go—I think a certain narcissism can lurk in the corners. But it is nonetheless true and important to note that Notley's move to venerate interdependency is a fairly standard feminist one, as feminists have been insisting for at least fifty years now that the *intersubjective* be considered as the true ground of human subjectivity, rather than fixating on a (hopeless) fantasy of complete individuation.

A blunter way to put this is that we were all born from a body, all born dependent on that body or on other bodies, and that despite our best efforts to repress, disavow, or outgrow that dependence, we remain dependent creatures to some extent all our lives. Notley's poem gets at this directly, by using the figure of a baby feeding on its mother as the one who "leans against," the one trusting for food to come out of another.

Feminists have had their work cut out for them, in that talking about dependency and reliance—especially using maternal metaphors—has rubbed a lot of people the wrong way, as many stereotypically feminized things do. (See current and forever debates on the horrors of the so-called "welfare state," a feminized and demonized condition if there ever was one.) But while "leaning against" might sound touchy-feely (as in, "We all need someone to lean on"), it's actually much more radical than that. At its most primal, it is about use—radical use. The baby makes use of its mother's body in a way that is pitiless.

The ethic here, if there is any, is not to continue, as adults, to make pitiless use of people. It is, rather, to come to grips with the fact that our basic dependency on others cannot be willed away and, further, that attempts to will it away in service of a fantasy of complete security, independence, or invulnerability can often have disastrous consequences, both individually and for a polis or state. In her beautiful and important book *Precarious Life,* Judith Butler explores how this fundamental dependency—she calls it our "precariousness"—might be a point of departure for political life.

Psychologist Adam Phillips, who sticks with a more psychoanalytical angle, puts it this way: "We depend on each other not just for our survival but for our very being. The self without sympathetic attachments is either a fiction or a lunatic. [Yet] dependence is scorned even in intimate relationships, as though dependence were incompatible with self-reliance rather than the only thing that makes it possible."

I like this quote. I like it because I'm also into—as a person and as a writer—"self-reliance." "I hate quotations. Tell me what you think." And just to show you how both impulses can coexist, sometimes virulently, within the same writer, here, again, is Notley, in an interview, describing what she terms her "poetics of disobedience":

It's possible that my biggest act of disobedience has consistently, since I was an adolescent, been against the idea that truth comes from books, really other people's books. I hate the fact that whatever I say or write, someone reading or listening will try to find something out of their reading I "sound like." "You sound just like . . . ," "you remind me of . . . ," "have you read . . . ?" I read all the time and I often believe what I read while I'm reading it, especially if it's some trashy story; intense involvement in theories as well as stories seems difficult without temporary belief, but then it burns out. I've been trying to train myself for 30 or 40 years not to believe anything anyone tells me.

So you can hold both impulses in the bowl. In my own writing life, I've often found myself very interested in dramatizing this coexistence—showcasing the situation we find ourselves in, in which dependence on others—or at least relation to them—is the condition of possibility for self-reliance. This is what I mean by "writing with, from, or for others"—the problem of performing relationality in a text. This is also partly why I titled one of my books *The Red Parts*, with the pun on "red" and "read"—the red parts being the parts of the Bible that Jesus speaks and that one might go to for consolation or guidance, and, alternately, "red parts" also being body bits, the insides, the guts, the female parts, the bloody truths that one's body, or the bodies of others, may hold.

Now, when I say "writing with," I don't mean collaborative projects. I'm generally way too much of an autocrat for such endeavors. Nor do I mean "writing for," as in, trying to please others with your writing; any writer worth his or her salt likely knows that one's writing—especially one's autobiographical writing—often doesn't please others, or at least not intimate others, and that one writes first and foremost to please oneself, and that's exactly as it should be and, further, that such an approach has no bearing on the work's generosity. Leaving the reader alone can be an act of enormous generosity, a vote for his or her autonomy.

Also, this relationality, this "leaning against" and its performance, is quite different from performing "influence," or an "inherited tradition," or some such. The leaning against I'm talking about doesn't mandate any reverence for your elders per se, nor any particular *kind* of relation or transmission. The leaning against I'm talking about takes place on a horizontal plane of action, not a vertical one. It brings one into the land of wild associations, rather than that of grim congenital lineage. It is a place, as Gertrude Stein would have it, in which "the difference is spreading."

While writing the books of mine that rely heavily on explicit, staged interaction with other texts—and here I'm thinking of *Jane: A Murder, The Red Parts, Bluets*, and my new book, *The Art of Cruelty*—I never conceived of myself as participating in some Oedipal anxiety about literary predecessors. Perhaps this is one of the great gifts of being a feminist: you're off the hook from all that crap. You know you don't really and truly belong in the canon club, so you're free to play. And the way that you play doesn't have to be stapled down into the dichotomy of reverence-for-daddy vs. disobedience-to-daddy, either. It can be something else entirely.

Listen, for example, to this great, negative review, written by Adam Kirsch, of Anne Carson's very brilliant *Autobiography of Red*. In this passage, Kirsch is trying to mince Carson's use of allusions by comparing her with that great poetic master Robert Lowell:

> For Lowell, historical and philosophical allusion are the very medium of his thought; he thinks through and in his examples, thus demonstrating in practice a coherent, and characteristically modern, attitude toward the past. He applies to each subject and personage his own voice and his own habit of mind, and the stain of a single personality emerges in the whole. For Carson, by contrast, the references to Heidegger, and to Stesichoros, and to Greek mythology, are not integral; they are showy, deliberately exterior to the main enterprise. They are ostentatiously announced and then simply left behind; any or all of them could be dropped without significantly damaging the Geryon narrative. Their purpose, then, is only to call attention to themselves; and it is the sterility of this learning, not the learning itself, that is injurious to poetry.

I love it—let's injure poetry! Let's get showy! Let's get sterile! I suppose it's possible that the allusions in *Autobiography of*

Red could be dropped and Geryon's story would remain more or less what it is, but the *book itself* would not remain what it is. For, like most of Carson's books, *Autobiography of Red* uses a weave of Dickinson, Stein, Woolf, Freud, the *Encyclopedia Britannica*, Yeats, *Fodor's Guide*, Pascal, Leibniz, Aristotle, Heidegger, Agatha Christie, Elmore Leonard, Walt Whitman, and even a porn magazine called *Balling from Behind* to ask a huge question that is of fundamental importance to me: to what extent can the words or ideas of others help us, or even save us?

It's a problem Carson returns to again and again—perhaps most painfully in the concluding piece of her book *Men in the Off Hours*, in which she writes: "My mother died the autumn I was writing this. And *Now I have no one*, I thought. 'Exposed on a high ledge in full light,' says Virginia Woolf on one of her tingling days (March 1, 1937). I was turning over the pages of her diaries, still piled on my desk the day after the funeral, looking for comfort I suppose—why are these pages comforting? They led her, after all, to the River Ouse. Yet strong pleasure rises from every sentence."

No matter that Woolf's words led her to the River Ouse. Pleasure arises from each sentence; for Carson, at this moment—and likely for us—that's enough.

Now listen to Carson's little red monster Geryon, the heartbroken hero of *Autobiography of Red*, sitting in his hotel room in Buenos Aires, looking out the window:

> He hugged his overcoat closer and tried to assemble in his mind
>   Heidegger's argument about the use of moods.
> We would think ourselves continuous with the world if we did
>   not have moods.

It is state-of-mind that discloses to us
(Heidegger claims) that we are beings who have been thrown
    into something else.
Something else than what?
Geryon leaned his hot forehead against the filthy windowpane
    and wept.
Something else than this hotel room
he heard himself say and moments later he was charging along
    the hollow gutters
of Avenida Bolivar.

In Geryon's hot and painful solitude, Heidegger fails him (even
though in his weeping and questioning, we can hear the pathos of
his hope that if he understood just a little more, he might be able
to mitigate his suffering). There is always this tension in Carson,
the tension between the declaration—made in the same sentence
in her book *Plainwater*—that "you can never know enough" and
"you can never leave the mind quickly enough." For Geryon suf-
fers, as many of us do, from the pairing of a fierce drive to obtain
knowledge and the drive to impede its progress—the drive to read
and absorb and be in conversation with the work of others and
the drive to ditch all the tortured mental wranglings behind and
"charge along the hollow gutters / of Avenida Bolivar."

This is as good a portrait of the balancing act between "leaning against" and "self-reliance" as I know.

What's more, this balancing act isn't just a writerly conun-
drum. It also characterizes the situation of desire, as the unre-
quited love plot of *Autobiography of Red* makes clear. Geryon
is in love with the much coarser Herakles, who, in one of those

awful breakup speeches we all dread hearing, utters to Geryon: *"Freedom is what I want for you Geryon we're true friends you know that's why / I want you to be free."*

To which Geryon memorably replies, in his mind: "Don't want to be free want to be with you."

"Don't want to be free want to be with you": this, too, is about as good a distillation of the problem of balancing human attachment with self-reliance as you can get. It's also a good distillation of Butler's much more complicated (but also beautiful) explication of the hard, often tragic, but understandable fact that it often strikes a human being as a better idea to "be enthralled with what is impoverished or abusive than not to be enthralled at all and so to lose the condition of one's being and becoming."

Spurred on by—of all people—Herakles's new boyfriend, Ancash, Geryon eventually does (literally) find his wings and take flight, and the story ends with Geryon's triumphant flight of freedom over a volcano. Interestingly, though, as Geryon prepares to light out, he pushes play on his video camera and shouts out, *"This is for Ancash,"* as he leaps out over the abyss.

The web of relation is everywhere, even in our flights of freedom.

However, as Kirsch's crabby review of Carson makes clear, the strategy of "leaning against" in writing is not universally revered. It's not guaranteed to win you fans or make you sound smart. To prove my point somewhat abjectly, consider the reviewer who said reading my book *The Art of Cruelty*, is "like reading a Tumblr full of tenuously connected posts—a tangle of other people's thoughts and observations." Or this review, about *Bluets*: "It's the sort of book you might read on an iPhone or an iPod. It is the sort of book to read while you're online, where the majority of us, if we admit it, operate these days. Leaving *Bluets*'s thread to check on your e-mail or your bank account is part of its aesthetic."

The first comment was meant to be a putdown; the second, not so much. But it seems to me no accident that both reference current technology. Both relate the art of assemblage to the way the Internet strings together quotes and ideas—the way a search engine thinks, or fails to think, as the case may be. If you are using the Internet to do your research—as I would imagine most writers today are—you will likely be held to similar standards, whether you participate in the technology or not. I sincerely wish that the fact that I don't even know what Tumblr is, have but the roughest understanding of Twitter, and have only seen a Facebook page in passing would disqualify me from these trends. But they don't.

I can even remember someone—I can't remember who—quipping that *The Year of Magical Thinking* was quite obviously Joan Didion's first book using Google as a research tool, and that you could feel it in her prose. The person didn't mean this in a good way. *Ouch!* I thought, when I heard this. (My next thought was *I'd really like to talk to Joan Didion about contemporary research and the writing process!* I mean, we're all in this together—we're all trying to figure out how to balance our brains, our technology, and our writing practices in the current moment in the most worthwhile way possible.)

But the truth is, the kind of intertextual writing I've been engaged with predates Tumblr. It is, in fact, as old as the sun. Most of the principal aesthetic models for my recent books, which include work by Roland Barthes, Joseph Joubert, Wittgenstein,

Goethe, Carson, Annie Dillard, Peter Handke, and Wayne Koestenbaum, either predate the Internet or are not written by avid
users or champions of it. But again, no matter; one cannot escape
one's time until one's time is done, and then, only maybe.

But, really, this is very good news for us all, at least for those
of us inclined toward leaning—and leaning heavily—on other
books or ideas for models and inspiration, because it means that
you don't often have to worry about ripping someone off. In most
cases, there are going to be huge, inevitable differences between
you and the person you are leaning against. And those differences
will ensure that your work isn't hopelessly derivative.

Many of my books have a kind of "ghost book," a book that
secretly—or not so secretly, as the case may be—stands behind
my book, not just as its muse, but often as its literal stylistic and/or
structural model. For my book *The Red Parts*, it was Peter Handke's
A Sorrow Beyond Dreams. For *Bluets*, it was Wittgenstein's *Philosophical Investigations*. In the case of *Philosophical Investigations*
and *Bluets*, the leaning against not only entailed working from Wittgenstein's ideas qua ideas but also involved lifting concrete sentence
constructions, locutions, and so on. But there are insurmountable
differences between us, which made the lifting productive.

First, there's the difference of genre: he's writing philosophy,
and I'm not. If you want to lean hard, pick something out of, or
tangential to, your field. With that difference comes difference of
intent: he's aiming to make sense to people who can follow intense
symbolic logic, and he's hoping to change the landscape of twenti-
eth-century thought; I am hoping to make some beautiful sentences
that will please me and express what I have to say and perhaps be
appreciated by a handful of other poets and "creative nonfiction"

writers. He's a mid-twentieth-century homosexual who was down-right phobic about sex (though he writes about bodily phenomena beautifully and obsessively); I came of age in a "liberated," confessional, decidedly American milieu, and have no problem affiliating myself with feminist and queer movements and writing.

I could go on and on. The point is, Wittgenstein and I are not going to have much overlap, so I could steal away.

And I did. While writing *Bluets,* I made a kind of wallpaper that actualizes what I mean by "writing with/from someone." It is a collage of index cards with sentence beginnings taken from *Philosophical Investigations,* such as "It is as if someone were to say," "Imagine that," "Let us now look," "Do not be troubled by the fact that," "For what goes on in you when you," "And now, I think, we can say:," "Suppose, however, someone were to object:," "It is—we should like to say—," "Are you sure—one would like to ask—," "It often happens that," "But you talk as if . . . ," "I will try to explain this," and so on.

Now, of course, if you steal like this, you have to *do* something to or with everything you've taken in—it has to come out the other end, it has to get chewed up by your own enzymes. You can't just pile other people's thoughts up, or even make a rough quilt or latter-day modernist collage of them and just cross your fingers that it's good enough. It won't be good enough. (I mean, it could be, depending on your goal, but let's just stay polemical for a moment and assert that it won't.) It won't be good enough without your having done the work of digestion, of transformation. You need to engage, and then perform, textually, the alchemy of your body thinking through another's body. The stakes have to be high; it has to matter.

So what does this digestion entail? How to make this leaning against something compelling, something your own? Here are but three ideas; obviously there are many more.

Pacing

PEOPLE OFTEN THINK of pacing as a narrative writer's game, as the word *pacing* would seem to imply that there's a set of facts or plot points that need to be brought "out" for the story to be told, and pacing indicates the speed and the order in which you parcel them out to the reader.

My experience with writing books like *Jane* and *Bluets*— which aren't quite narratives, but aren't quite *not* narratives, is that pacing is still key. The question becomes how do you make the performance of this *leaning against* into a page-turner? How do you showcase the hinge of self-reliance and relationality in a compelling way?

Take, for example, this poem from *Jane*, called "The Gap":

> *Consciousness*
> *does not appear to itself*
> *chopped up in bits,*

> William James
> once said.
> *It appears to itself as continuous.*

But there can be
holes in time
the mind tries

to ignore, holes
that perforate
the felt of

the night sky.
An aching gap,
James said, trying

to describe
the space made
by a lost word.

To fill it up
is the destiny
of our thoughts.

What transpired
for five and
a half hours

between Jane
and her murderer
is a gap so black

it could eat
an entire sun
without leaving

a trace. *Listen*
hard enough,
James said.

You can hear
the rhythm
of the ache.

You may have noticed that this poem hangs on a quotation.
Several of the poems in *Jane* hang on a quotation, be it from
my grandfather, my mother, the police, a true crime book, William James, or Jane herself. The trick is to give the quotation its
due, but also to handle it kind of roughly, like it's an ingredi-
ent in your batter and you've got to meld it into your making.
You've got to hear the music of someone else and marry it
to your own. I sometimes call this "sound-stitching." In this
particular poem, the stakes of this stitching have to do with
pairing the violent rupture that occurred on the night of Jane's
death with my own rupture of the James quotation—with my
packing of my inquiry about Jane's last night on earth into his
rumination on consciousness, and then the resolution of both
thoughts together.

Forms of Address

QUITE LITERALLY, YOU have to ask, Who is my book talking to? (Note that this is not the same question as Who's going to read it?—not the same at all!) Who are you sharing all this knowledge with, and why? What's the vector, what's the temperature, what's the tone?

A quote from Wayne Koestenbaum, from a conversation he and I once did for the Poetry Project, speaks to this quite well. In it, he describes a formative scene of writing for him, to which I think most of us can relate: "I'm reminded of the time some psycho girlfriend of mine (decades ago) answered a long rhapsodic letter I'd written her with this terse, humiliating rebuff: 'Next time, write to me.' One command, on a tiny slip of paper, tucked into an envelope. Derrida hadn't yet written *The Post Card*, so I had no context for my failure as a letter writer, as a sociable being."

"Next time, write to me"—you are and you aren't writing to someone, that's the rub! But the trick is to use that tension as an engine rather than as a confusion (or source of offense!). I've often heard it said that certain books (actually, maybe all books) have to teach their reader how to read them. Often this is done in the opening bits. Here, for example, are some pieces from the opening of my book *Bluets*:

1. Suppose I were to begin by saying that I had fallen in love with a color. Suppose I were to speak this as though it were a confession; suppose I shredded my napkin as we spoke. *It began slowly. An appreciation, an affinity. Then, one day, it*

became more serious. Then (looking into an empty teacup, its bottom stained with thin brown excrement coiled into the shape of a sea horse) *it became somehow personal.*

2. And so I fell in love with a color—in this case, the color blue—as if falling under a spell, a spell I fought to stay under and get out from under, in turns.

3. Well, and what of it? A voluntary delusion, you might say. That each blue object could be a kind of burning bush, a secret code meant for a single agent, an X on a map too diffuse ever to be unfolded in entirety but that contains the knowable universe. How could all the shreds of blue garbage bags stuck in brambles, or the bright blue tarps flapping over every shanty and fish stand in the world, be, in essence, the fingerprints of God? *I will try to explain this.*

4. I admit that I may have been lonely. I know that loneliness can produce bolts of hot pain, a pain which, if it stays hot enough for long enough, can begin to simulate, or to provoke—take your pick—an apprehension of the divine. (*This ought to arouse our suspicions.*)

. . .

8. Do not, however, make the mistake of thinking that all desire is yearning. "We love to contemplate blue, not because it advances to us, but because it draws us after it," wrote Goethe, and perhaps he is right. But I am not interested in longing to

live in a world in which I already live. I don't want to yearn for blue things, and God forbid for any "blueness." Above all, I want to stop missing you.

You'll note that in this section, there are a lot of "you's"—the "you" that's actually "me," the you that's "you, the reader," the "you" that's a particular other (a beloved in absentia), the "you" that's rhetorical, as in "one."

In short, the form of address doesn't have to be the same throughout—the "you" of the piece, if there is one, can be a multitude of different "you's"—but you have to control the tone, the demand on your reader. Is it urgent, is it melancholy, is it lonely, is it trying to be read, is it trying to hide, is it trying to disseminate knowledge, is it trying to simply get done with the thinking and saying so it can charge out "along the hollow gutters of Avenida Bolivar"?

Bookending (or not)

WHEN COMPOSITION TEACHERS are trying to teach students how to use quotations in analytical papers, they often instruct them that every quotation used must be "bookended"—i.e., first introduced, then commented upon by the student writer. Clearly, this isn't the case outside of such spheres. And yet the concept is still a useful one for me, insofar as one's employment of or disobedience to the procedure highlights the fact that there are times to let others speak for themselves and have the last word, and times when one really needs to talk back, explain, refute, add on. In the poem "The Gap," for example, I thought William James deserved the last word. In those opening bits from *Bluets*, I felt it important to dispute the Goethe comment, and then to end, "Above all, I want to stop missing you," because I wanted to torque the register in the final moments. And here's a later moment from *Bluets* that uses a pause to have it both ways:

88. Like many self-help books, *The Deepest Blue* is full of horrifyingly simplistic language and some admittedly good advice. Somehow the women in the book all learn to say: *That's my depression talking. It's not "me."*

89. As if we could scrape the color of the iris and still see.

At first, the women in the self-help book get the last word. Letting #88 end that way leaves open the possibility that they're right, that that's really how depression works, that that's really how one can and should get better. Then the somewhat crabby narrator, who is, in some ways, trying to hold on to her depression, comes in and squashes the idea, equating it with a form of self-mutilation or blindness. But the space between the two propositions leaves it open as to who's looking at it right—which is as it should be, as I'm trying to get at fundamentally unanswerable questions: What is the "true" self? What is the nature of its afflictions? What remains of the self once those afflictions have been subtracted or cured?

Lastly, on the topic of bookending (or not): such a practice is predicated on the idea that one is interested in dramatizing the differences between one's words and those of another, rather than intentionally blurring their authorship. Obviously there are, and have been throughout time, many writers who've found it fruitful to angle their practice toward this blurring. There have also been, in recent years, many spirited defenses of literary plagiarism (those by David Shields and Jonathan Lethem come immediately to mind, as does the work of John D'Agata, albeit at an angle). There's something weird about this conversation, however, which has kept me from wanting to enter into it. I'm not going to get into it now, but my instincts tell me it has something to do with gender, and gendered histories of originality and erasure. But I leave that subject for a different time and place. My main point is that I'm presently more compelled by writing that showcases the various ways one might "lean against" than that which aims to obscure the process. I believe that our words, ideas, and thoughts are in essence shared, that they surround us like an ocean, and that writing can be like dragging a cup through those communal waters and seeing what you net. But the sometimes difficult, sometimes ecstatic (and sometimes both) burden of trying to navigate between self and other cannot be easily dismissed, nor should it be. We literally come into being as a knot of self-reliance and dependence, and so we continue on, each and together, on the page and off it.

THE EXPERIENCE IN BETWEEN:

Thoughts on Nonlinear Narrative

ADAM BRAVER

Stevie Wonder's Hotel Room

I ONCE READ that when he toured from city to city, Stevie Wonder insisted on staying in identical hotel rooms. Apparently, doing so made it that much easier for him to navigate his way through them, always knowing everything would be in the same place: the towel bar, the desk, the phone, the bed, the closet. I appreciate that there are times when there's a need for predictability. For order. We each need a framework in our own way. But I also know that the place where experiences actually happen, where they have their real meaning, is in the spaces between order and predictability, both in terms of what occurs in those spaces and their relationships to other events. I'm willing to bet that Stevie Wonder didn't navigate his way through those rooms in the same order. I imagine each day's circumstance brought its own path. The sameness of the room was more about touchstones. Something to ground him, and to give him context at the moments when it seemed like it all could get away from him.

The Collage of Local News

I USED TO love to watch the local news when I'd land in an unfamiliar city. Spread across a hotel bed, remote in hand, I'd tune in to the network affiliate's version of the news. It was like a guidebook. The broadcasts were half-hour lead-ins into the national news, with the packaged glitz of the parent network in the titles and music, yet glazed with an indescribable "local" quality to the video that I guess we call "low budget." But it wasn't the novelty of the broadcast style that drew me in; it was seeing the way the city was portrayed. It always gave me a better sense of where I was.

I can barely watch local news anymore. The stations have all changed their approach to programming. With their nightly themes of house fires, street violence, and car crashes, broadcasts are merely formulated plotting, with the cunning of the sleaziest genre novels, for which we instinctively know each storyline and its outcome before it even starts. Now, no matter what city I'm in, after a half hour of local news, I realize I could be anywhere.

But there didn't used to be a predetermined narrative. A broadcast was organized according to what were believed to be the most noteworthy stories of the day. The city hall scandal. A ribbon cutting. An octogenarian's gift to the city. The birth of a giraffe at the zoo. The overall narrative was presented with a controlled randomness, held together only by a recognizable beginning and end. The stories, almost episodic, fit together, but not quite. At best, the anchor might transition between pieces by suggesting we were going to a "lighter note." But to an outsider, these broadcasts offered a collage of the best and worst of the community—a narrative collage, if you will—that not only showed the disparate parts of the town I had just entered but also, through piecing together those disparate parts, gave me a complete experience of where I was.

It's Basic (Part 1)

IT'S THE PIECES—their arrangement and the spaces left between them—that tell a story. It's about navigating an unfamiliar world with some sense of predictability, while accepting that underneath the surface meaningful experiences are happening in the most natural, least explanative way. That's all I'm really getting at here.

And Then . . . And Then (Part 1)

I WAS BORING myself. My own pages were putting me to sleep. The manuscript in question was *November 22, 1963*, for which I'd recently conducted a lengthy phone interview with Aubrey Rike. On the day of John F. Kennedy's assassination, Rike was sent with a hearse to Parkland Hospital, where he not only witnessed the calamity and confusion taking place within the emergency room, but by pure circumstance experienced it with a shocked and befuddled Jacqueline Kennedy seated beside him.

It was exhilarating, that interview. The details. The way Rike lit Mrs. Kennedy's cigarette; over forty-five years later still recalling his trembling hands. The contradiction of being on the inside and the outside at once. His visceral description of the meal he ate immediately after leaving Parkland. I couldn't wait to get it all on the page. Yet when I wrote it out, keeping the chronology as precise as Rike had, the draft, later called "The Casket," fell flat. All the details were there. The narrative was well paced. Yet no matter where I trimmed, how much I reduced the prose, tightened the language, it continued to read to me as *And then . . . And then . . . And then . . . And then*.

Searching for Something New

THERE'S A MOVIE I like to watch for inspiration: *The Mystery of Picasso*, directed by Henri-Georges Clouzot. Through a reversed filming technique, as well as something I assume is stop-motion animation, the film shows Picasso at work, documenting the evolution of his creative process, primarily from the perspective of the blank paper and canvas, almost as though Picasso is drawing on the camera lens. Several works are produced throughout the movie, from watercolors to sketches to oils (all of which would be destroyed after the filming). What sticks out most, why I come back to the film, are the moments when the pieces first take form—sometimes as an amorphous block of color, sometimes with recognizable subjects, and sometimes just as a series of lines. Watching the artist's opening moves is thrilling—a little like shaking a gift box and trying to determine what the present is. But inevitably, and this really is where I'm heading, Picasso will change direction, adding a figure or shape that suddenly alters and shifts the anticipated image. And as these new forms develop, the picture itself begins either to explode into something completely different or, more typically, to shape into a new perspective on itself—perhaps maintaining the meaning and feeling that has been inherent to the piece from the start, but rejecting the familiarity of expectation.

"When I paint, my object is to show what I have found and not what I am looking for," Picasso said in a 1923 interview with Marius de Zayas. "In art, intentions are not sufficient and, as we say in Spanish: love must be proved by deeds and not by reasons. What one does is what counts and not what one had the intention of doing." Perhaps that explains my draw to this film. In their initial states, many of the pieces begin in that place Picasso is "looking for," a familiar terrain, a kind of base camp, if you will. But when we end up at the place he's found, we understand that much of it is the result of a variety of ideas and impressions happily colliding into its own unique and meaningful experience (to reiterate Picasso's quote: *What one does is what counts and not what one had the intention of doing.*) While we all seek something new in the familiar, we are so often burdened by our instincts of mimesis. But even harder—harder than reminding ourselves not to feel fulfilled by the skilled re-creation of the familiar—is how to create a new kind of experience without completely dismissing or demolishing the essence of what we know. On some level, the intent should be to disregard initial intentions. A favoring of exploration over expectation.

And Then . . . And Then (Part 2)

THE FIRST THING I did was to get out a pair of scissors and a roll of Scotch tape. Then I sat Indian-style on my office floor, the pages of "The Casket" surrounding me. The chronology had to be broken. Maybe not reimagined, but at least re-seen. Somehow the focus on propelling movement in the cause-and-effect narration of the actual sequence of events was making the piece lose its potential power and energy. I cut ten sheets into close to forty small scraps. Some of the pages were dissected into as many as six parts; others only sliced in half. Then I took the liberated scenes and placed them beside others that might have some kind of kinship. Again, this wasn't about looking for chronological relationships; instead, I was searching for that "something else" that inherently connected them. It felt like trying to make a jigsaw puzzle without ever having seen the picture on the box. For some sections, it was obvious when two fit together. They shared an image. Had a clear juxtaposition. Told a complete story. Or clearly were complementary ideas. Other times, I'd force parts together, trying to believe they might fit, but ultimately realizing they didn't connect. When I found a good match, I'd tape the sections together. In most cases, the new sections were stronger but incomplete. And because "The Casket" essentially became something new, there arose a whole host of narrative challenges and issues that ultimately had to be solved by further research, revision, and/or rewriting. The process was slow and meticulous. It was a collage taking form. And as I began to see those episodic experiences coming together to tell the story on their own terms (not unlike those old local news shows), my sense of boredom shifted to a sense of excitement.

Two Simple Formulae

1. Because I'm generally talking about characters, essentially human beings, the equation is always thus: *the sum total of a series of intersections = a single experience.*
2. The follow-up equation then might be: *the sum total of experiences = truth.*

Experience

I WANT AN experience. I want to feel something, not just re-create a series of events that might, at best, offer some new vantage point on a familiar scene. I want the experience of the road trip, not just the pushpins on the map and the measurements of the legend. I can accept that art and literature are often about giving order to the chaos of the world, and I'm not arguing against that. But the idea of order has a wide berth. And order doesn't always equate to linear narrative.

An experience (at least in the literary context I'm using) is a reaction between two things: the point where all the disparate factors that make a single moment meet and the untold space around that axis point. What I mean is this: while the progression of time may be linear, as well as the series of events that happen within that progression, *experience* is not about cause and effect. A million things at once are happening. There are the politics. The weather. The chance encounters. The coincidences. You name it. Every moment that appears to be singular is always being bombarded from a plurality of angles.

Just as we need to recognize those seemingly disconnected moments in "real life," we also need to find them in our writing. To allow an experience, the writer must concede the space between the random events and the point where they meet. And that space, I believe, is not something to be colored in and fleshed out. It is something left best untouched, something to marvel at—how this seemingly isolated, innocuous coincidence of events becomes uniquely meaningful. We must resist the urge to try to fill in the gap with analysis. That space *is* an experience. To try and explain it is, well, *explanation*. As a reader, I want the experience. Yes, it can take more work to recognize, feel, and understand what's really taking place, but, ultimately, it's more satisfying, because it means I'm participating in the narrative. And somehow that brings more understanding and meaning than a thousand explanations.

It's Basic (Part 2)

TO RATIONALIZE AND bring justification to every experience only kills it. It deflates the impact of any emotional power. I mean, would you rather be in love, or would you rather just sit around and talk about it?

Stevie Wonder in the Round

IN OCTOBER 1986, I saw Stevie Wonder perform in Sacramento at what was then called Arco Arena. The show was staged in the round, meaning that Wonder and his band were on a circular stage that slowly rotated throughout the entire concert, never pausing. It brought to mind both a merry-go-round and a turntable. The intention seemed genuine, a way to reward everybody with a full, unobstructed view at one time or another (or the contrarian's position: a way to ensure everybody had equally bad views at one time or another). Positioned all the way to my right, the band kicked off with the synthesized horns of "Sir Duke," not reaching my section until the song went into the bridge, and then soon gliding to the left during the final chorus. It felt awkward; the musicians always turning away, even as they played midsong, their whole bodies entrenched in the groove, seemingly unaware of any shift in direction, as though performing on a regular proscenium. Wonder, also, appeared unaffected by the transience. As the stage moved, he stood, as usual, shifting between keyboards, reaching for a harmonica, and, at points, he'd strap his *keytar* (a guitar-shaped keyboard) around his neck and be led up to a microphone. Sometimes, if the musicians faced you at just the right moment, you might catch a smile on his face, an unscripted call out to the lead guitarist, or a grimace on a high note that had never happened in rehearsal. For me, the dedicated focus on the physical structure of the event (one that we were supposed to be wowed by) robbed me of any musical connection. It was alienating. But I couldn't help but imagine that for Wonder, it was much like his hotel rooms—from his perspective, the concern was not about the mechanics of the staging; it was in knowing where everything was so he could make music. Who cared about the direction and the pace of the spinning stage? As long as he could navigate between instruments and knew what song was next, then he could just play music, free to find the unknown experiences still to come between the notes.

ON THE MAKING OF ORCHARDS

AIMEE BENDER

SEVERAL YEARS AGO, I was reading Dante's *Inferno* with some friends, and there was one line in particular that struck me. It was the Pinsky translation, Cantos XI, and the line is "God / Has as it were a grandchild in your art." I wasn't quite sure what that meant, but in the notes in the back, Pinsky says the structure goes more or less like this: there was God; God had a child and that child was Nature; then Nature had a child and that child was Art, making Art God's grandchild.

I think that is an extremely beautiful statement; it is so precise and interesting and shapely. The quote links art and nature in this very, well, natural way. If you happen to believe in God, then there's some supreme head of it all (or if you run it backward it's a gorgeous definition of God—Art coming from Nature coming from a grand shapely unknown), but if you don't find that useful, you can move down the line anyway and see that nature operates under certain rules of DNA and biology and that art operates under similar rules but in its human-made metaphorical way. That when making art, what we're trying to do is create something with this natural, unimposed structure.

In a class I taught last year at Tin House, we talked about diversity in nature a lot—about how if you take a category, any category, the range is amazing. Trees, dogs, clouds. Every morning, students would go up to the chalkboard and draw on a different theme, for example, bugs, and we'd look at all the bugs in a row—grasshopper, butterfly, ant, spider—because they are all such different shapes. Or we would draw deep-sea fish, because deep-sea fish are also wildly surprising different shapes. The writer Jay Gummerman once reassured me about plot by reminding me that "there's structure in nature." And there is also such variety. There are boundless options, options with integrity. All trees do not look like the tree that a kid draws of the stick-with-puffy-cotton-ball. Evergreens, palm trees, oaks, Japanese maples—what different forms! We can have that expectation for fiction, too. All stories do not need to have the same arc, the same progression of character, the same twenty-page Times-New-Roman beginning-middle-end movement. We can allow our writing to form its own shape. David Shields has said that you don't want to pour your writing into some kind of mold; it should be the form that it is. But I love the idea that the *reason* a piece of writing should take its natural form is because art is nature's kid. For me, that reinvents a word we use often in workshops, the word *organic*.

And these thoughts led me to fruit. If we look at the process of how fruit is made on a tree, we can see that it mirrors the process that happens in fiction, inside a sentence, inside a paragraph, or inside a whole story. We're hoping the writing will bear fruit. But fruit does not happen in some quick way; it happens through a gradual process. It's not as if a seed pushes out a stick that then bears an apple. Right? The seed grows into a trunk, which grows a branch that grows a blossom that bears fruit. The definition of fruit is "any product of plant growth useful to humans or animals"—"useful" being an interesting word—"the edible part of a plant developed from a flower," and "anything produced or accruing; the product, result, or effect; *the fruits of one's labors, something coming to fruition*." This is all just another way of talking about process, about development.

What interests me about this process in terms of teaching, and my own writing, is that I often see two things happen— first, a writer (myself included, of course) rushes to the fruit, to the dramatic moment, to the meaningful epiphany. In those cases, the result feels like plastic fruit. That's what is meant when readers say, "It's not earned." The ending is too tidy, or fast. It has not gone through a genuine movement; it has skipped somewhere in the process from seed to branch to blossom. And the opposite happens all the time as well, which is that something *is* developing, the writer's building his story, he's going seed to branch, he's going branch to leaf, and then he stops. And you feel like something needs to be pushed more; there needs to be a hint more development at that stage, but the writer is holding back, is not letting the seedlings of what he's developed blossom. This is not to say the writer should spell everything out! He can still leave it open, can let the reader come in and do that work, but sometimes the process stops long before a reader can even get her hands dirty with the pleasurable job of finding the fruit. Sometimes the writer just hasn't stayed in the piece long enough to make adequate space for a reader to enter. And if fruit is something "useful," something that we can take away, something that is our nourishment, that we live off, when a story doesn't get to that stage, we don't have a satisfying response to it—we have something, but not quite enough of the story, of the character, to take with us, to keep with us. We don't have enough there to haunt us.

Now, what fruit is, per story, is obviously going to be very, very different, because, as we know, there are lots of different kinds of fruit. There's the cantaloupe, there's the blackberry. Aesthetics will vary.

ON A RELATED note—I'm not trying to encourage you to overstate. You can certainly go too far and overstate what you think is going on with your character or story. That is not what I mean by fruit, and this essay is not about that. This is about staying with the moment on the page, staying with what you've built. A good friend of mine is an actor and she told me that one of the most useful comments she ever got in an acting class was the teacher said that the lucky thing about being an actor is that you also happen to be a person. You're a person and that's helpful, because you are playing one, too. You have something very basic in common with your character. And I think there's something similar in this idea that whatever you're building in the scene is full of what you've already put into play; seedlings are already in place and you can start to look at them, to turn them around in your hands. What's helpful about writing is you happen to be writing.

GERTRUDE STEIN WROTE a book called *How to Write*, which is a bit difficult to read, of course, but also pretty wonderful. In it, she says, "A sentence is not emotional a paragraph is." She says this over and over, being that she's Gertrude Stein: "A sentence is not emotional a paragraph is." "A sentence is not emotional a paragraph is." In a lecture of hers about narration, she elaborates on this. She talks, in her roundabout and yet somehow very precise way, about succession (and in her windings isn't she kind of the queen of succession? of subtle changes that make a progression?), about how one sentence follows another, and how sentences have to obey certain rules of structure, whereas in a paragraph you begin to build something in a different way. At the end of this talk, she says:

> A sentence is inside itself by its internal balancing, think how a sentence is made by its parts of speech and you will see that it is not dependent upon a beginning a middle and an ending but by each part needing its own place to make its own balancing, and because of this in a sentence there is no emotion, a sentence does not give off emotion. But one sentence coming after another sentence makes a succession and the succession if it has a beginning, a middle and an ending as a paragraph has does form create and limit an emotion.

In other words, the larger context forms the shape. If a sentence has an emotional impact, which of course it does all the time, it does so in large part because of its placement against other sentences, and because of how, almost musically, the emotion will land on a paragraph or scene or moment or white space or word. I think Stein is talking about fruit here, in her own way.

ONE MORE ASIDE—I really like thinking about all this but I do want to add that however much we think about it, it's always going to be a somewhat mysterious process. It's fun to try to figure out what goes into the process of writing, but my wish is generally that you take in what interests you, and then pretty much forget it. I wouldn't really recommend that you sit with a notebook by your side later, at your computer, and meticulously try to pull some fruit out of your writing. That can easily make the work feel clunky and pressured. My hope is that these obser- vations just go into your primordial brain soup and that maybe you will push a sentence, a scene, a story, a moment, consciously or not, just because you are more deeply *in* it.

HERE ARE A few examples to try to make this all a little clearer.
    This is by Basho, one of the great haiku masters. It is, I think, the smallest version of something very, very complete that moves swiftly through the fruiting process:

> Even in Kyoto—
> hearing the cuckoo's cry—
> I long for Kyoto.

"Even in Kyoto" plants the seed, places the reader; "hearing the cuckoo's cry" is the seedling, creating the atmosphere; and then, the blossom: "I long for." We're moving toward the fruit—what is it he longs for? "Kyoto." He longs for where he already is. Or he longs for a memory that is unfindable in real life. It's not a punch line—it's a natural build that takes us somewhere unexpected; he has captured something both elusive and exact.

If we move into a slightly larger space, we see how fruit can be borne within a paragraph or short passage. In *Lolita*, Nabokov builds his incredible, articulate paragraphs with shockingly interesting sentences that burst forth; things are happening and fruit is blossoming at every moment. At the start of a paragraph fairly early in the book, the narrator, Humbert Humbert, talks about a photo taken by his aunt of him, his young love, Annabel, and others sitting around at a café. He spends a few phrases just describing the photo—"her thin bare shoulders," his "moody, beetle-browed" face. Then, he gives the context: "That photograph was taken on the last day of our fatal summer and just a few minutes before we made our second and final attempt to thwart fate." He's changed the game on us—we thought we were just enjoying a photo, but it turns out to be a very important photo, a marker of sorts. He then goes into describing what happens after he and Annabel run off, in sentences of the most gorgeous language and such surprising succession: "There, in the violet shadow of some red rocks forming a kind of cave, had a brief session of avid caresses, with somebody's lost pair of sunglasses for only witness. I was on my knees, and on the point of possessing my darling, when two bearded bathers, the old man of the sea and his brother, came out of the sea with exclamations of ribald encouragement, and four months later she died of typhus in Corfu."

We could probably study this for hours, it's such an incredible stretch of prose, but for the purpose of this essay, I'll say that one of the things I love most about it is the momentum. We start with the snapshot, with time frozen. We see Annabel; we see Humbert. How easy it might've been to end shortly after that, or after the line about the fatal summer. But instead Nabokov fills in the moment, swiftly, deeply, with the lost sunglasses both anchoring the scene and adding a hint of despair, because no one but Humbert will ever have this memory, all of this undercut by the surprising, funny entrance of the two bearded bathers, and his wonderful brief step into describing them as mythic creatures, larger than life. So we're with him, with his disappointment at the thwarted attempt, and then we're led directly—within the same long sentence!—to her death. A frustrating and classic adolescent moment leading to total loss and death. That ending phrase slams it down, shakes the reader, and suddenly the whole paragraph breaks open; we can see the loss, and why he's talking about all this in the first place, and the gloriousness of his youth and life and adoration of Annabel, and then the quick, brutal ending.

"A sentence is not emotional. A paragraph is"? Nabokov demonstrates this idea hugely here. Another crucial part of the fruit and musicality of this passage is the subsequent chapter break, the white space at the end. There's a gap in which we have a moment to try to digest what we've read, but it is also somewhat indigestible. Nabokov has moved through time so fluidly, it's all happening before our eyes and faster than we can even keep up with, and the white space gives us a moment to feel, briefly, this punch in the gut, which then we also may continue to feel in faint reverberations throughout the book. Fiction does this kind of time skipping so well; more, I think, than any other art form.

The Moviegoer, by Walker Percy, is, in part, about a young man trying to figure out what he's doing with his life. In perhaps my favorite passage in the book, the scene initially feels focused in one direction and then it turns. First, Walker plants the seed, sets the scene, in a conversation with the main character's aunt, who says: "'Last week at Great Books I had a chat with old Dr. Miner. I didn't bring your name up. He did. He asked me what you were doing with yourself. When I told him, he said it was a shame because—and there was no reason for him to say this if it weren't true—you have a keen mind and a natural scientific curiosity.'"

After that, we get a little background, a little history, from the narrator: "I know what she is going to say. My aunt is convinced that I have a 'flair for research.' This is not true. If I had a flair for research, I would be doing research. Actually I'm not very smart. My grades were average. My mother and my aunt think I am smart because I am quiet and absent-minded—and because my father and grandfather were smart."

Then he moves the story into an active moment, a clear memory:

I tried research one summer. I got interested in the role of the acid-base balance and the formation of renal calculi; really, it's quite an interesting problem. I had a hunch you might get pigs to form oxalate stones by manipulating the pH of the blood, and maybe even to dissolve them. A friend of mine, a boy from Pittsburgh named Harry Stern, and I read up the literature and presented the problem to Miner. He was enthusiastic, gave us everything we wanted and turned us loose for the summer.

But then a peculiar thing happened. I became extraordinarily affected by the summer afternoons in the laboratory. The August sunlight came streaming in the great dusty fanlights and lay in yellow bars across the room. The old building ticked and creaked in the heat. Outside we could hear the cries of summer students playing touch football. In the course of an afternoon the yellow sunlight moved across old group pictures of the biology faculty. I became bewitched by the presence of the building; for minutes at a stretch I sat on the floor and watched the motes rise and fall in the sunlight. I called Harry's attention to the presence but he shrugged and went on with his work. He was absolutely unaffected by the singularities of time and place. His abode was anywhere.

As the passage continues, the narrator tries to undo this stunning discovery of beauty by ending the paragraph with a throwaway line about chasing a girl for the rest of the summer. But of course he can't undo it—the beauty has happened, to him and to us. He makes us think we're going one way, with his background in research, and the vocabulary of science, and then there's that shift, and suddenly you feel as though you know this character more deeply, and, in fact, this is the character that you've been following throughout the whole book—one who is wrestling with this exact sensitivity in himself. By allowing the prose to swerve, Percy finds the fruit and lets us in on a whole new level.

Alice Munro is a writer who delivers fruit at the most unexpected moments and delivers it big time—something will grow and happen in her stories, but it is never what the reader expects. She is a master innovator of plot in this way. In a scene from her story "Chance," a young woman, Juliet, is traveling on a train by herself for the first time, and she's really reveling in a new independence. She's coming into her own. Then this guy sits down next to her and he's annoying; he's one of those annoying people who sit down, and you want to read your book, and he wants to talk to you and chum around. So they have an exchange that in itself develops and is very interesting, and Munro masterfully tucks the smaller fruit of this scene and its payoff inside the larger fruit of the full story. Through the progression of their dialogue, we see that it gets to the point where Juliet is feeling so pressured by this man's desire to be her buddy that she actually does something she's never done before, which is excuse herself. She says, "'I do want to read. I think I'll go to the observation car.' And she got up and walked away, thinking she shouldn't have said where she was going."

During this interaction, there is a turn in the character, and that turn in the character propels the next event in the story. And with that next event, all these other moments start to line up, and there's a much bigger thing that happens as a result. Everything is creating a certain pressure on Juliet. But what's so satisfying is that the scene in itself is compelling and developed. You could easily have a scene in which someone comes and is annoying and then leaves. Or, I think, a much easier, much more common option is to have a scene in which an annoying person comes, and the main character kind of mutters something and maybe looks out the window. Right? It would be very tempting to have her at that moment stare out the window and have him give up and maybe read his own book, to almost make the scene but then skip it, to dampen the tension, to go to that leafy stage and not make the fruit, which for me is the moment she decides she's going to leave, does leave, and the consequences in her mind (and in the story) of that action.

The short-short is a mode in which the fruiting process can build swiftly throughout the entire piece. Barry Yourgrau's short-short stories are all present tense, so he doesn't time skip, but he moves in ways unexpected—like satisfying, not-annoying dreams. Here's Yourgrau's "By the Creek":

I come into the kitchen. My mother screams. Finally she lowers her arm from in front of her face. "What are you doing, are you out of your *mind!*" she demands. I grin at her in my bermudas and bare feet. "It's okay," I tell her in a chambered voice through my father's heavy, muffling lips. "He's taking a nap, he won't care." "What do you mean he won't *care,*" she says. "It's his *head.* For God's sake put it back right now before he wakes up." "No," I tell her, pouting, disappointed that her only response is this remonstration. "I'll put it back in a while." "Not in a while, *now,*" she says. She moves her hands as if to take the head from me, but then her hands stammer and withdraw, repulsed by horror. "My *god,*" she says, grimacing, wide-eyed. She presses her hands to her face. "Go away! Go away from here!" "Mom," I protest, nonplussed. But she shrinks away from me. "Get out of here!" she cries.

I stalk out of the kitchen. Hurt and surprised I plod heavily up the stairs. I go into my parents' bedroom. I stand at the foot of the bed. My father lies on his back, mercifully unable to snore, one arm slung across his drum-like hairy chest in a pose particular to his sleep. I look at him. Then I back away, stealthily, one step at a time, out the door. On silent, bare feet I steal frenetically down the hall, down the front stairs and out the front door. On the street I break into a run but the head sways violently and I slow to a scurrying walk, until I'm in the woods. Then I take my time on the path, brooding, my hands in my bermuda pockets. I come to the creek and stand balancing on dusty feet on a hot, prominent rock. The midafternoon sun lays heavy, glossy patches on the water and fills the trees with a still, hot, silent glare. A bumble bee drones past, then comes back and hovers inquiringly. I get off the rock and stoop down, bracing the head with one hand, and pick up a pebble. I get back on the rock and fling the pebble at the creek. It makes a ring in the water. Another ring suddenly blooms beside it. I look around at the path. A friend of mine comes out of the trees.

"Hi," I say to him. "Hi," he says in a muffled, confined voice. He stops a few feet from me. "You look funny," he says. "So do you," I tell him. I make room for him on the rock.

"Where's your dad?" I ask him. "In the hammock," he says. "Where's yours?" "We don't have a hammock," I tell him. "He's in bed."

Half an hour later there are half a dozen of us standing great-headed at the side of the creek.

Let's examine the development here.

First, we're thrown in. The mother screams. Something's up. The seed is planted.

Then we discover it's something about the narrator's head. His father's head. The seed grows into the wonderful slow development of him seeing his father, the consequences of this magical happening ("mercifully unable to snore"!), and its logical stance in Yourgrau's world.

Is that enough? Not really. It's interesting, but if he stopped here it'd be a kind of still life of weirdness.

So he goes outside. Something's blossoming. He's on his own. He's by the creek. We spend a little time with what it's like by the creek, building the blossom, allowing the moment. Still, though, it isn't quite enough.

And then another kid shows up. How? We see the first sign of him in the creek, another circle blooming beside the first circle. Someone else skipping stones—what a great entrance. And, he's wearing his father's head too, which we find out in a subtle way. What continues to be so crucial is this matter-of-fact acceptance, the agreement that this is the way it goes in this world, and all the room that gives us to interpret.

The story could easily end with the two of them, but there's a pause, and then that final line, which widens and deepens the story. What would happen if that last line wasn't in the story? It becomes almost anthropological there, and invites us to enter the story and wonder with him, and that, in my mind, is where it fully fruits. (Also, the word "great-headed"? How oddly, unexpectedly, right.)

And finally, sometimes the fruiting process is a much slower, more gradual process. I was looking at passages in *Gilead* by Marilynne Robinson to see if I could include one here, but that novel works through an accrual of scenes, some of which bear fruit and many of which don't. Instead, they are building, building, building until the end of the novel, where there is very much a blossoming and a fruiting and an incredibly moving close. If Stein says, "A sentence is not emotional a paragraph is," perhaps you could also say that sometimes a chapter is not emotional, a novel is. That the progression can take place over the course of the entire novel. The sequence of chapters and the build give you the fruit. A chapter itself may often be emotional, yes, but overall it is more about how the chapters work against and with each other that brings the piece to that place where we "take something away."

THERE'S AN EXERCISE I'll do sometimes with a class in which we'll start with a word; I'll give everyone a word, and they'll write based on that word, and as they're writing I'll interrupt often and tell them to write more on the setting they're developing. I'll stop the process again and give intrusive instructions about developing the character in the setting, and on and on. The purpose of this is to allow the development of the fruit that is already in seedling form on the page. There can be an urge and an anxiety to skip ahead, to get to the action, to get to plot, or to go to the familiar. But plot is a process, and its beginnings can come from very subtle and unexpected places. Story movement and form are going to feel false if they do not happen from some kind of progression, even if (and this is important) the writer is not aware of this process in the moment, even if, as with the Nabokov excerpt, the events happen fast. When people say a storyline is contrived, it's often because something has been anxiously shoved into place as opposed to following its natural development.

A FEW YEARS ago, I listened to a rabbi give a talk and she was explaining what a blessing is. It is a naming of something, she said. What you are blessing already has to be latent in the person, otherwise it doesn't mean anything. But if it is (latent), and you bless what hasn't yet come forth—the fruit—it is a very powerful action. Think of your writing as bestowing a blessing. I'll leave you with that.

GET A JOB:

The Importance of Work in Prose and Poetry

BENJAMIN PERCY

I MARRIED INTO a farm family. For four generations, in the northwest corner of Wisconsin, outside the wooded hamlet of Elk Mound—where the Packers rule and cheese is never far from the hand and the blasting white winters weaken you into something half-alive—the Dummers have risen at 4:30 every morning to milk their seventy-five Holsteins and to disc and plant and harvest their thousand acres of corn and soybeans.

Every few months, my wife and I make the five-hour trek from our home in Iowa to visit; the last time was in May. After we heaved our suitcases inside and collapsed in a travel-weary daze at the kitchen table, my father-in-law came in from the barn, shook my hand, and said, "Corn up?"

He wanted to know where he stood compared to Iowa farmers. He wanted to know whether the rain had let up, whether the tractors had grumbled through the fields, whether the first green shoots were springing from the furrows. I could say with certainty, "Yeah, corn's up, ankle-high," because I had looked. Because I knew he would ask. Just as I know he will ask in July, "Tasseled out yet?" and in September or October, "Harvesting?"

He's a dangerous driver; as we putter around Elk Mound, his attention flits so often from the road to the fields that we'll frequently find ourselves straddling the yellow line or skirting a ditch. With one hand on the wheel, he'll list off who owns what land, who needs a new combine, who's selling out to a developer ready to hammer together a subdivision. He'll brake along the shoulder to ogle a new manure spreader.

I admit to having felt puzzled when I first met him, when he asked me whether anyone in my family farmed, when every conversation somehow cycled back to chores or machinery or crop yield. It took me a few years to get used to his way of seeing the world. Now I anticipate it—and think of him every time I pass an implement dealer or gaze out over a rust-colored spread of soybeans after an autumn freeze.

And this is what so many beginning writers fail to realize— the same thing I failed to realize when I first met my in-laws— that your way of seeing the world bends around your work.

We spend the majority of our adult lives hunched over a desk in a hive of cubicles, or fitting together auto parts in a factory assembly line, or scraping charred burger off a grill as a line cook, or stuck in traffic limbo somewhere between the boardroom table and the La-Z-Boy recliner. And yet in most of the student stories I read, work is mentioned only in passing or is absent altogether.

Whether or not we like it, work defines us. Work dominates our lives. And we have an obligation, in our prose and poetry, in the interest of realism, and in the service of point of view, voice, setting, metaphor, and story, to try to incorporate credibly and richly the working lives of our characters.

Point of view, as we well know, is the filter through which a reader observes the story. Any number of things will influence the perspective—whether a character was beaten or coddled by his parents—whether a character comes from Libya or Canada or Uzbekistan—whether a character can rack two hundred pounds on the bench or barely hoist a gallon of milk—whether a character has loved or grieved or betrayed or killed—whether a character lives in a time of war or a time of peace—whether a character is a rosy-cheeked seventeen or a gray-haired, glaze-eyed eighty—but chief among them is a character's job.

Let's say our character is a fashion model. Call her Georgiana. Forget making her complicated and three-dimensional. For the moment, we'll happily wallow in stereotype. Georgiana walks into a room. What does she see? Every reflective surface? A mirror, a window, a knife. Anything she might use to check her hair, her lipstick. Or maybe she accounts for the lighting, standing far from the chandelier that drags shadows across her face but close to a table lamp that gives off a soft glow. Maybe she inventories the designer labels. Maybe she eyes up the competition—determining who is skinnier, who prettier. Maybe she clacks her high heels across the hardwood floor to make certain everyone turns to look when she first walks through the door.

The introduction to the Showtime series *Dexter* is similarly exaggerated. As the opening credits roll, the titular character (a serial killer played by Michael C. Hall) goes through his morning routine: a razor nicks his neck, an egg cracks like a skull, ketchup bloodily spots his plate, a tie nooses around his neck. The possibility of violence is everywhere. Harold Crick, played by Will Ferrell, is no less a caricature in *Stranger than Fiction*. Crick, an IRS auditor of infinite calculations, is hardwired to notice numbers, to make formulations—calculating the number of steps it takes to get from his apartment to the bus, determining the most precise and efficient way to knot a tie, load a dishwasher.

There are many versions of Harold Crick in Joshua Ferris's white-collar novel *Then We Came to the End*. The characters work in a Chicago advertising firm, and every day everyone wears some variation of the power suit or the long-sleeve button-down with ironed chinos. The characters are assigned to cubicles and glass-walled offices. They carry out the same actions over and over and over again, filling out spreadsheets, calculating earnings, sitting through endless PowerPoint presentations. And their story is told in first-person plural:

> We were fractious and overpaid. Our mornings lacked promise. At least those of us who smoked had something to look forward to at ten-fifteen. Most of us liked most everyone, a few of us hated specific individuals, one or two people loved everyone and everything. Those who loved everyone were unanimously reviled. We loved free bagels in the morning. They happened all too infrequently. Our benefits were astonishing in comprehensiveness and quality of care. Sometimes we questioned whether they were worth it. We thought moving to India might be better, or going back to nursing school. Doing something with the handicapped or working with our hands. No one ever acted

on these impulses, despite their daily, sometimes hourly contractions. Instead we met in conference rooms to discuss the issues of the day.

This point of view might come across as gimmicky if not for the circumstances: the work destroys individual identity and the employees become part of a capitalist collective, a conformist hive. Boardroom rhetoric infects the voice: "benefits astonishing in comprehensiveness and quality of care," "printing errors, transposed numbers," "call now and order today." This is what too many meetings and instruction manuals and water-cooler conversations will do to you.

Every now and then a character will break away from the "we," and every now and then the sentences will buck their slow, formal cadence with a "fuck" or a "damn," and every now and then the characters will yearn for something else, something brighter than the harsh glow of the fluorescents overhead. But only for a moment. The voice is as buttoned down as an Oxford pinstripe.

Compare that to the untrammeled voice and frayed-edge blue-collar perspective of Kevin McIlvoy's "The People Who Own Pianos":

We never can find their fuckin houses.

We get a set of shit directions there, a different set of shit directions back. Okay, we've got an attitude about the goddamn load no matter what we're told it is—grand, baby, standup, damaged, used, good used, or good—fifth or first floor, basement, attic, narrow or wide staircase—the kit or the whole coffin—it's the same to A.D. Moving.

We carry it out into the light beyond the lighted, decorated, dimwit room we rearrange, rip, gouge, and nick all we want on our way out. Make way, we say, make way—words that give use rights greater any day than the owners', am I right?

The piano mover encounters setting as a series of tight hallways, narrow staircases—and as economic indicator. The world is broken down according to the haves and the have-nots. The people who own pianos are the people who have hot tubs, stainless-steel ovens, top-shelf scotch in the liquor cabinet, oxblood wingback leather chairs with gold buttons. Like Ferris, McIlvoy uses the first-person plural. However, in this case, the "we" is there to distinguish the *us* from the *them*. The people who move pianos are not the people who own pianos. And like Ferris, McIlvoy supplies us with plenty of insider jargon—when he describes a grand versus a baby, the kit or the whole coffin, mummifying the sound, amputating the legs—making us trust the author, the credibility of the story.

But unlike Ferris, McIlvoy strips away all formality from the voice, the sentences laden with profanity, comma splices, and paratactic speech patterns meant to capture the rough-edged everyday chatter of somebody who might drag up a stool next to you at the bar. In the texture of the voice, I hear boots clomping up and down stairs, a heavy load gouging plaster—and there is music in this, like a country song writ large.

Sometimes I like to think of myself as a referee—dressed in my black-and-white stripes, whistle dangling around my neck—racing up and down the sides of student manuscripts. Every now and then, I will make a series of complicated hand gestures, screech my whistle, and say, "Point-of-view violation!" This is because the writer, after establishing a first-person or close-third point of view, has violated the constrictions of that perspective. In the first few sentences of a story, you establish a contract with your reader. You have violated that contract if you, say, leap from the gaze of a beachside sunbather to that of a pilot in a plane streaking overhead.

Nor, tonally, can you build baroque sentences when the mind of your character is empty, his life unadorned. Her voice cannot sound like white lace and gold trim when her home reeks of cheap whiskey and wood smoke. The trucker does not have a laugh like a booming bassoon. The trucker laughs like a hot tire ripping apart at eighty-five mph. The kindergarten teacher has Crayola blue eyes, *not* gunmetal blue eyes. Unless, of course, the title of the story is "Mrs. Snodgrass Finally Snaps." Point of view corrals description and metaphor—and the job determines point of view.

Consider Brian Turner's poem "At Lowe's Home Improvement Center":

> Standing in aisle 16, the hammer and anchor aisle,
> I bust a 50 pound box of double-headed nails
> open by accident, their oily bright shanks
> and diamond points like firing pins
> from M-4s and M-16s.

The poem's soldier-narrator hovers between two worlds, not at peace and not at war, not a marine and not a citizen, not a part of the United States and not a part of Iraq. A fan reminds him of the rotor wash of a Blackhawk helicopter, a cash register drawer has the rattle of chain gun, a dropped palette booms like a mortar, paint pools in the aisles like blood. He cannot separate himself from his work. It is there, at every turn, imprisoning him.

It is *your* job to do the required research that will bring the language and tasks and schedule and perspective of your character's work to life.

A job, too, sets story in motion.

It is a job in Walter Kirn's *Up in the Air* that leads Ryan Bingham to the woman who will make him crave something more substantial and authentic than his single-serving lifestyle.

It is a job in Philip Levine's poem "You Can Have It" that yellows the hands and hunches the backs and shortens the breath and the life of two brothers who spend their lives sliding ice blocks down chutes, stacking crates into boxcars.

It is a job in Susan Orlean's *The Orchid Thief* that sends her into the swamps of Florida and a plant-poaching underworld in which she glimpses passion for the first time.

It is a job in Margaret Atwood's *The Handmaid's Tale* that punishes Offred, a concubine, and makes her ultimately join a resistance faction that challenges the male dictatorship of her country.

It is a job that frames and sets into motion every element of your story or essay or poem—and it is *your* job to do the required research that will bring the language and tasks and schedule and perspective of your character's work to life. Google can only do so much for you. The library can only do so much for you. You need to write from the trenches.

One way to approach this is to channel your past. The age-old writing maxim is, after all, *write what you know*. That's what Mike Magnuson did with his novel *The Right Man for the Job*, drawing upon his time working as a repo man in Columbus,

Ohio. That's what Pam Houston did with her memoir, *Rough Guide to the Heart*, writing about her experience as a river and hunting guide. The job doesn't have to be extreme—doesn't have to be romantic or dangerous or grotesque—to be compelling. You could do the same with your time making swirly cones at Dairy Queen or nannying for two snot-smeared little trolls or folding skinny jeans into perfect sharp-edged piles at American Eagle.

So you could write what you know. The problem is, of course, that some people don't know shit.

In which case, flip the rule on its head and know what you write. Tom Wolfe never walked on the moon, but that didn't stop him from publishing *The Right Stuff*; he spent years on the book, researching, interviewing astronauts, visiting Cape Canaveral, making sure he secured every detail about the manned space program. I've never worked as a taxidermist, but a few years ago, I wrote a short story about one called "The Killing." I visited a taxidermy studio, stroked my hand along the polyurethane forms, clacked the glass eyeballs around in my palm, and sniffed the formaldehyde. I spent several days working with the employees, eavesdropping on their conversations, taking notes on the peculiar insider lingo you can never glean from Wikipedia.

Writing is an act of empathy. You are occupying and understanding a point of view that might be alien to your own—and work is often the keyhole through which you peer. Before I met my wife, before I heard my father-in-law's alarm blare at 4:30, before I saw him wax a tractor and peel a cowl off a birthed calf and shrug off an oil-stained set of coveralls and combine corn until midnight and toss straw bales into a barn loft and tear through pasture in a mud-splattered ATV, a barn was nothing but a red blur out my car window. Now, after observing him and helping him work—the two of us scraping manure from the barn floor, picking rock in the fields—I understand the greater ways in which our work defines our character.

Get a job.

SHORT STORY: A PROCESS OF REVISION

ANTONYA NELSON

LAST SPRING, I taught an undergraduate fiction workshop that differed significantly from any other workshop I've taught or taken: I tried to have my students mimic the process I go through when writing a story. In most workshops, students are charged with creating two or three short stories in the course of fifteen weeks. But I myself have never written three short stories in a semester—at least, not since graduate school, when I was in a workshop that demanded it of me. I don't know many writers for whom three stories in fifteen weeks is a habit, but somehow in workshops it's become the procedure. The fact that that doesn't replicate my own process seemed sort of weird after a while.

So I decided I would make an experiment with my students to have them go through the full process of creating a piece, taking the story from inception through stages of revision to its eventual polished ending. I insisted that they undertake the process of writing that I myself undertake. I dictated the stages, it's true, but I am the teacher, and that's my prerogative. It proved for an interesting semester, and I'm going to refer to what happened in the class as I present the process here. I'm also going to illustrate the process with a hypothetical story I wrote as I moved through the stages of the exercise with my class. So these are the threads being braided or woven or tied in knots in the course of this essay. I hope it doesn't get confusing.

On the first day of class, I had my students write a five-hundred-word piece about an event that actually happened to them and that they understood was a *story*, something they'd tell in a bar or on a plane or to a friend. I had them write it in the first person and I capped it at five hundred words. The thing that I wrote, when we sat down to do this, began, "When I was five, my family was in a tornado," which is true. That happened to me. My family was inside a car, in Kansas; all of us were there, including my little sister in utero. There are a lot of us, five children and my mom and dad. My little brother and I were three and five, and we were in what is called the "wayback" of the station wagon. We were on our way home from dinner at a restaurant in early September, and we saw lightning strike. We pulled into a parking lot and watched roofs ripped off houses, rain pouring down hard, and the wires from electric poles snapping on the ground. In the parking lot—this was at a strip mall—there was a Baskin-Robbins ice-cream parlor, and I can still remember the image of all the people behind the plate glass licking their ice-cream cones and looking out at us in our car in the parking lot, a parking lot that was *full* of cars, yet ours was the only one that had people in it, and ours was also the only one that was lifted up and turned over by the tornado—twice. With us inside it. We all survived.

You can see how this would strike a person who'd gone through it as a story worth telling, right? That's a story! So there's my autobiographical event. I had my students write about their own autobiographical event, some nugget of narrative that they intuitively understood had meaning. I wanted the event to be autobiographical because it's important that writers have an investment in and an attachment to their stories, as well as some authority over them. They need to write what they know, what they care about. The tornado, in my family, was a defining event in our lives. I told that story for years and years and years.

But the autobiographical event needs to be given some freedom to become art, so the next step is to allow that story fictional leeway, because art is best if it's not hampered by the constraints of factual anecdote. The next step for my students was to occupy the point of view of a third-person character related to the event and not the person *they* were in relationship to the event. They had to posit another character to oversee the story. In this way, the material is approached from a new angle, opening up the possibility for fiction.

In my own case, I didn't want to be stuck in the point of view of a five-year-old. My pressing concern in 1966—when I was that age and in that tornado—was that I not wet myself. It was *deeply* important to me that I not pee my pants while we were in the ambulance. That's a five-year-old's concern.

And so, for my story, I would occupy the point of view of my father, or *the* father, *he*, *him*, the third-person character who was driving the car on the night the tornado happened and who was, oddly enough, the same age then as I am now, which puts me in the curious position of having intimacy with that point of view. I'm more likely to be the driver of a car full of people these days than I was then, obviously, and now I understand what it must have been like for my father to be the parent driving a car that's then tossed into a tornado.

When I began occupying the point of view of the character who was my father, I realized that I didn't want to set the story in 1966 because I don't know what it was like to be an adult in 1966. I would set the story in the *now*, so that I could write from the point of view of an adult *now*. Would I place it in New Mexico or Colorado, where I live? No, because we don't have very many tornadoes in the places where I live. I would keep the story in Kansas. So I'm combining the fictional, in that I inhabit the story from the point of view of a third-person character who isn't me, with the factual, putting the story in a place where the event that I wish to write about actually happened. This merging of what is personal and what is fictional, what is factual and what is made up, starts happening for me in the process of writing a story.

That was a thousand-word draft. Every time my students went through a revision, I upped the word count by five hundred. It was an arbitrary, but manageable, number. By creating multiple drafts (by my insisting that each revision was its own draft and had only to attend to the requirements laid out for that draft), students revised with a single objective each time. The clarity of writing with a single objective seemed helpful. All the stages were accompanied by literature that provided examples, so we could talk about the stories they were reading, the writers they were modeling. And with every draft, they workshopped the pieces in small groups that changed with each revision so that they had new eyes on their material at each stage.

The third step—I've got a point of view, and I'm invested in this story I'm creating—is to put some sort of *clock* on the story. What is a clock, in the vocabulary of story making? It can be any of a variety of things, but ultimately it is a shaping device through which you signal to the reader the time they have to spend with your characters. For instance, the clock can be a road trip. If you set characters in motion on page one and they are traveling across the country, the story would be over by the time they arrive to their destination. Using a literal clock, the clock that dictates the day, is an impulse people seem to resort to very naturally when they sit down to write. There are many stories that begin with someone waking up—you've probably been tempted to write one of those yourself. It makes sense to me that consciousness, or the sudden arrival of awareness, would be a starting point for a story, which suggests then that darkness or nightfall, sleep and the release of consciousness, would mean the end of a story. The clock can be the time line of an hour, a day, a weekend, a summer. A ceremony is a clock; a ritual is a clock. Starting with the preparations for a large party—in the instance of, say, Clarissa Dalloway in *Mrs. Dalloway*—of course leads to the book ending with the party.

You can also use a clock in the way that Alice Munro claims to construct stories, with the notion of there being a house through which someone is wandering, so that the shape of the story becomes a house whose rooms must be visited and understood. You can use Joseph Campbell's hero's journey, the duration of a friendship, or the stages of grief as a clock. Anything can become a clock. You just need to find one that suits your story. I recommend you look to the works you love and see how they begin and end and how the construction and movement of time gives them some sort of shape.

For the clock in my story, I asked myself, Do I want to write about the day of the tornado itself? Or am I interested in something other than that? Writing about the actual tornado reminded me of that not-as-fascinating-as-it-might-sound conflict: man vs. nature, and while the dramatic business of being tossed around in the car *was* fascinating, it doesn't really lead me, here and now, to a story I'd be likely to write. I would be more inclined to dwell in the aftermath. Here's why:

In the true aftermath of our tornado, there was a photograph that some AP photographer took of me and my dad being hauled to an ambulance. It appeared on the front page of our local newspaper—the *Wichita Eagle*—which correctly identified us. But when the photo appeared on the wire and then in stories around the country, the caption read, "Young Toni Nelson with unidentified man." For weeks following the tornado, my dad kept getting these weird letters and phone calls "identifying" him. People would call and say, "That's my long-lost brother." Or husband. Or son. All over the country this "unidentified" man, who was my father, kept being identified. Wrongly. He was none of those people. And that's kind of cool to me, and it makes me think, as an adult looking back, *Well, there's something to interrogate.*

Of course, another factual thing is that my mother was pregnant, and so in the interval between September, when the tornado happened, and October, when my sister Julie was born, we wondered if the baby was going to be okay. Everything indicated she would be okay, but it was nerve-racking. So I think that is the clock I would put on that particular story—the aftermath of the tornado, the immediate effects of anxiety, my character's concern about what his wife is going to experience and whether the baby will be normal while receiving these odd updates on who he is from around the country.

My students had to attach a clock to their stories that made some kind of sense with the material they were writing about. It had to have some bearing; it had to be something that was built into the anecdote they had started with.

I then asked my students to go through the material they had written thus far and identify the props and objects that would be of use to them in the story. The props and objects draft was a draft of detail-making. Some of the props might become red herrings, but some might be of use. The students' only charge was to chronicle what was (or could become) useful objects in their stories. In my own story, that photograph became a kind of prop or tangible object to take advantage of, to play with, and also perhaps to be used to dictate the terms of the clock in the story. I also had the bashed-up car, the ice-cream cones being licked by people behind a window, and an unidentified man who's being misidentified.

The next step was to determine the protagonist's age. In addition to imposing a clock on a story, determining the proper age for the protagonist is, I think, one of the story maker's biggest decisions. Imagine a time line, a line whose beginning is a person's birth and whose end is that person's death, then imagine significant mile markers along the way. These are markers that have their sources in several factors: physical, psychological, sociological, biological, intellectual, et cetera. They are not firm markers, but approximate ones. At certain moments in our lives we face transitions. Ideally, the central character in a short story is in a transitional situation. If you can sync your character with a sociological or otherwise traditional transitional moment, you will have a more powerful position from which to illustrate your character's dilemma. So it's important to know the age of your protagonist, because the transitions that happen to us are sometimes of our own engineering, but oftentimes, they are products of a cultural or biological or social transitional moments, and if you can match those up with your character, you're going to have a story that makes use of the proper time for the proper transition. Or, conversely, you will create a powerful distortion because the transitional moment is inappropriate; it's wrongly placed. For example, sexual knowledge that comes at age nine or ten is not properly placed and so becomes a disrupted transitional moment.

Here are some basic transitional ages. Age three or four: your first memory, the first time you begin owning your life through an ongoing series of memories. That seems to me quite significant. Five years old begins a sort of social transition. You become a kid who goes to school. Eight years old—well, if the kids are like mine and you drive the way I do, they start pointing out to you how you're speeding and it's very upsetting to them because you're breaking the law and they know you are, and they can't reconcile that their good mom would be doing this bad thing. They turn into little cops in your car. William Faulkner's story "Barn Burning" makes use of that particular transitional age. The child protagonist is, roughly, eight or nine years old. His brother is twelve, and his other sibling is younger, about five. The story is *his* story precisely because he's at a moment when he must either commit to the family's way of living, which is to burn down barns and then go to some other place and get accused of burning down barns but always get out of it, or he has to say that his father burns down barns, in which case he's taking a stand against his father. For him, this is a hugely conflicted moment, because he knows what's right by law, and he knows what's right by family, and they aren't the same thing. For him, this is a conflict that's genuinely of consequence. The five-year-old sibling does not care, cannot see it, and the twelve-year-old has already stepped over the line. The story could only be happening to this eight- or nine-year-old child. A transitional moment—cognitive, social, whatever—is *very* useful in situating your story.

Let me illustrate this another way. If you said to somebody, "This is a story about a son who lives with his mother," there's no obvious conflict built into that situation, or expectation about it, until you name an age. He's ten: of course he lives with his mother. He's fifteen: naturally he lives with his mother. He's twenty-one: well, who knows, he might go to college someday. He's thirty-five: he really ought to move out of his mother's house. He's fifty-seven: there's something very wrong with him. Or with his mother. Or both. What age will give a story the most hinging power? Let's say you want to write about a woman who's worried about not being pregnant. She's thirty. Okay, I'm sympathetic to a point. Age thirty-five, I'm a little more sympathetic. Age forty-one? I'm worried for her. You've increased the pressure of the situation merely by aging her a bit. So consider a character's time line. You're probably going to write only one story about this character; make sure you've got her at the right transitional moment to tell her story.

Maybe every story ought to be a coming-of-age story, in that coming-of-age stories are always about the reluctance or difficulty of passing into the next phase. The most common passage in a coming-of-age story is adolescence, but there are many other passages. The best coming-of-age stories are ones in which a character has to make a passage but regrets or fears or fights against having to do it, because once you've reached the other side, once you know what you don't want to know (this seems to me to be the crux of every Hemingway story; the guy resists— *No, I don't wanna know that. No, I don't wanna know it.*) you can never *un*know it. You pass a point of no return.

So back to my own example: I've decided my father character is in his middle age and he, like my own father, is an atheist. After the tornado, people would say, "You're so lucky. You're so lucky." And my father's reply was, "How is it lucky that of all those empty cars in the parking lot, our car was the only one picked up?" What's interesting to me about this is that the fact of being selected, it seems, by a tornado, in a parking lot *full* of vehicles, and being turned over and dashed about, might give an atheist some pause. The middle-aged father character, having long established a sense of self and beliefs, is suddenly challenged by the thoughts that maybe there *is* a God, maybe he is an "unknown" person, is it time to change his life? And so this would become, for me, a way of inhabiting the character further.

We were in week eight or so of the class at this point. I asked my students to take the most recent draft and introduce a world event into it. Something from the world had to come into their story. It could be as simple as sending the characters to a Halloween party or as complex as having the characters evacuate after Hurricane Katrina. I asked them to insert something of the world into the story to see how that gave them an outside influence for their characters to do battle with. When a world event enters a story, it creates a new dynamic. Oftentimes my own work has been accused of being too insular, too negligent of the larger world, too much about the privacy and smallness of family. So in an effort to challenge myself, I decided I would use the events of 9/11 to inform my story. The actual tornado had happened at the same time of year, September, so the decision was somewhat organic. Let's say that the tornado happened on September 5 and then the World Trade Center gets attacked on September 11. How is that useful to me in terms of navigating some new material in the story? Well, I think—and this is purely speculative; I've not actually written this story—it would be interesting to consider the ways in which an attack on America driven by religious fervor might affect a man who doesn't believe in God. As in: what is the power of belief? That might be something I'd begin speculating about in the story if I decided to use 9/11. And if 9/11 were too dramatic an event to enter this story, I might set the story on the anniversary of 9/11, a year later. Or maybe the five-year anniversary would further defuse the overwhelming power of 9/11. This is the stage my students really resisted, and in a couple of instances, it didn't make a better draft of the story, but by and large, it did.

I next asked them to divide the elements of their stories into what I call *binaries*. I've quit thinking about short stories as having the traditional conflicts as taught to me in junior high school.

Then, it was explained as three choices: man vs. man, man vs. nature, or man vs. himself. It has never been useful to me as a writer to think about conflict that way. But what *is* useful to me is to start identifying the opposing forces that are providing a piece with some sort of energy or tension. And that, I think, *is* conflict. In Flannery O'Connor's "A Good Man Is Hard to Find," for example, there is the Misfit, who has a very concrete understanding of the Bible, and there is the grandmother, who has a very abstract adherence to the tenets of the Bible. There is the empty sky, and there is the ground occupied by the characters. There is the sense of violence and the sense of passivity, travel and stasis, the right thing, the wrong thing, Jesus and the devil, the living and the dead. Faithfulness and a lack of faith. And so on. These are oppositional forces, and they create tension and conflict within that story. So I asked my students to start making sure they had binary forces at work in their pieces. If they supplied one part of the binary, they needed to have the other part ready. They needed to understand that there would be something missing if they didn't fulfill the binary—that tension requires both parts.

The next draft involved creating a traditional story arc, that quite reliable Freytag's Pyramid you probably also were taught about in junior high school. I want to emphasize that story arc, the idea of rising action, is not about plot, in my experience of writing, but about the writer's ability to keep creating tension and meaning by upping the ante and raising the stakes as the story proceeds.

An example of this is "Sonny's Blues," by James Baldwin, which takes place over about a two-year period and has no discernible plot—none. It's a series of recollections, events, encounters, but it does not have a plot, or not what you would call a plot. Yet the reader's investment in that story grows and escalates because of the ways in which Baldwin shapes the story. First, he shapes it with the theme of music. If you trace music throughout the story, the first instance of it being mentioned is a "very complicated" yet "very simple" whistle that the narrator hears on the stairs of the school where he teaches—a boy is whistling. The next instance is music coming from a jukebox in a bar that the narrator passes. This is followed by a mention of music he heard in the past, when his father was playing a guitar. And the next reference, also in the past, is to a piano that his brother, Sonny, played, but that he didn't hear, because he was off at the war. The next instance is a combo of musicians on the street that is improvising; he's hearing it from a bit of a distance but he can see that people are moved by it. And the final instance of music is when he is at a bar listening to Sonny play improv with a group—perhaps the most complex and difficult situation of music that exists. So there's an escalation that accommodates this arc, and it is very deliberate and it accrues power over the course of the story—from the high, thin whistle somebody is just blowing from his mouth to, at the end, a jazz combo performing brilliantly and beautifully. That's one of the ways the arc in that story is accomplished.

There are other ways, but I'll just mention one other, which is the presence of Sonny himself. The story begins with the narrator on a subway train, underground, reading about his brother in the newspaper. That's how distant they are from each other. The next instance is that he runs into a friend of Sonny's. So it's some connection to Sonny, but not a literal connection, not a real connection. The next instance is that Sonny writes him a letter. The next instance is that Sonny gets out of jail. The next instances are told in flashbacks. And in the next instance the narrator and Sonny are together, looking out a window, and Sonny tells him it's so horrible to see all that passion out there on the street. Yet the brothers are still not as intimate as they need to be for the story to fulfill its arc. The final instance is when they're at the bar and the narrator realizes he is hearing Sonny's music fully for the first time. It's hugely powerful, because of this narrative arc. Baldwin is counting on the reader's ability to take in narrative constructed this way, even though it's not plot-driven. It's very important to me to emphasize this, that the shapeliness of fiction almost always depends on the presence of an arc, and it's not simply a plot-driven device; it's the ways in which the story creates meaning and emphasizes and amplifies. And it has to work on the reader sneakily or he or she won't be persuaded. Alongside a traditional story arc, I asked that students also make sure they had at least three scenes (conforming, I suppose, to the notion of beginning, middle, and end).

Toward the end of the semester, because they had read some Donald Barthelme and George Saunders and John Cheever's "The Swimmer," I asked my students to try something crazy in their stories to see what happened. Would it be a better story if it were told in the second person? Would it be a better story if it were told in the present tense? Would it be a better story if it were told in reverse chronological order? Would it be a better story if it were told from the dog's point of view? Do something crazy, I told them, and see if that shakes something loose that you have yet to think about. Make something magical happen in it. Let there be something bizarre. Only one in about one hundred short stories—that I read, anyway—successfully uses some of these quirkier mechanical moves and gestures, and that seemed about right for the class. Only one student made something unrealistic or distorted from a straightforward, conventional story work to his advantage. But it worked really well. He had written about a pet store in a storm, and everybody starts starving, and they all go a little nuts, and the story was well served by allowing the characters a kind of craziness and the animals a bigger sentience than you would think animals would possess. So for him, that was great. For the rest of us, it didn't work out so well. For example, how would my own story profit if I alternated the point of view with that of the in utero sibling? What was my future sister (my character's future daughter) experiencing during the tornado? It would be compelling to write, but probably wouldn't serve the realistic terms of the story.

And then, finally, on the last day of class, I received their stories. The pleasure of reading those heavily revised pieces was singular in my teaching experience. The authors and I alone knew the scenes and anecdotes that had engendered each piece. The manipulations were impressive; the shapeliness of each was solid. The stories were all, to a person, durable and thought provoking. Of course, there is almost always more work to be done. That was never emphasized to me in grad school. I was always just churning out yet another story for workshop rather than going back and truly investing in one story for a lengthy period of time and dedicating myself to making it somehow better. If you are not invested, truly invested, in the fiction you're making, it will show. The reader will not be invested in it either. Oftentimes when reading fiction, I feel a detachment on the part of the writer toward the material, but when I'm reading the work I love best, I understand that there's something at risk for the writer in it, that something, whether it's autobiographical or not, matters to that writer, and that *thing* really makes some difference. I was tired of my students' work not seeming to matter enough. I wanted them to be at some risk. What my students took away from that experience is what I hope you take away from this report on it: the work you're writing is worth your attention and it really is in revision that you're going to find something meaningful and useful.

THERE INTERPOSED A _____:

A Few Considerations of Poetic Drama

MARY SZYBIST

SOME OF THE earliest advice I received about writing poetry went like this: stop telling stories. One teacher patiently explained that there is simply not room in a poem to explore the lines of cause and effect so central to fiction. Another offered a memorable variation on T. S. Eliot's words, advising: "Plot is the bone you throw the dog while you go in and rob the house."

It has taken me a long time to ask: What kinds of stories *are* poems good at telling? I think it is fair to say that poetry tends to specialize in interior dramas, but even if we accept this distinction, how do poems effectively set up the *outward* occasions—the stories—of those interior conflicts? How a poem sets the stage matters. In this essay, I want to consider one dramatic setup that has proven particularly useful to poets. Let's call it the drama of interposition.

Interpose: from the Latin *inter*, meaning "between," and the French *poser*, "to place." To interpose: to insert between other elements; to place between (in space or time); to come between, either for aid or for troubling. For aid, as in, "the prince interposed and made peace." For troubling, as in "an interposing thicket blocked their way." And sometimes both for aid and for troubling.

Traditional storytelling is about obstacles: what the hero must overcome to save the city, to get the girl, et cetera. Poetry is often about obstacles too, though they often take the form of quiet interruptions. Just as a hero advances toward his goal until an enemy gets in his way, the speaker of a poem is often moving toward something—a beloved, perhaps, or an expected destination or outcome—when something else drops in. Emily Dickinson's famous poem is a ready example:

> I heard a Fly buzz—when I died—
> The Stillness in the Room
> Was like the Stillness in the Air—
> Between the Heaves of Storm—
>
> The Eyes around—had wrung them dry—
> And Breaths were gathering firm
> For that last Onset—when the King
> Be witnessed—in the Room—
>
> I willed my Keepsakes—Signed away
> What portion of me be
> Assignable—and then it was
> There interposed a Fly—

With Blue—uncertain stumbling Buzz—
Between the light—and me—
And then the Windows failed—and then
I could not see to see—

Just when it seems that there is nothing to stand between the speaker and her death, "There interposed a Fly—."

What makes this a promising drama for a poem? (Granted, Dickinson could make great poetry out of any occasion, but I think it is not an accident that this scenario resulted in one of her most anthologized and best remembered poems.) First, the story line is not an elaborate one: we have an intimate sense of who, where, and when. Dickinson gives away and dispenses with the plot in the first line: "I heard a Fly buzz—when I died—": that is the whole story. It is a simple story of intrusion.

As to what is being intruded upon—that may be a more complicated matter. To better understand this, let's compare this death scene to another one that Dickinson describes in a letter to Jane Humphrey in 1852. Dickinson muses: "Bye and bye we'll be all gone, Jennie, *does* it *seem* as if we would? The other day I tried to think how I should look with my eyes shut, and a little white gown on, and a snowdrop on my breast; and I fancied I heard the neighbors stealing in so softly to look down on my face-so-fast asleep-so still—Oh Jennie, will you and I really become like this?"

The still, fast-asleep face, the white gown, the hushed grievers: many of us might imagine our own deaths with hopes of similar tranquility. It is a fairly conventional vision—which may be the reason why Dickinson doubts the veracity of the scene she describes: "Will you and I really become like this?"

The speaker of the poem has the same basic idea of how death is *supposed* to go. Graceful, dignified, the speaker proceeds toward death in an orderly way: she wills away her possessions, surrounds herself with loved ones, and looks toward the light. So it is not simply that the fly interposes itself between the speaker and death; the fly interposes itself between the speaker and her ideas about how death is supposed to unfold. This is the kind of shift that I am proposing is so rich in a lyric: when a speaker is following a given path and its protocols, something is interposed that prompts reseeing and reevaluation. The almost humorously mundane housefly upends the steady trajectory toward an exalted "King."

If things are interposed for aid *or* for troubling, the fly in Dickinson's poem seems a straightforward example of a troubling intrusion. The speaker can no longer continue the experience that she and others *thought* she was having. And yet, the interposition of the fly moves her away from the inherited and predictable script and gives her a chance to see and hear the experience that she is *actually* having—which is complicated, "uncertain," "stumbling." The actuality of death is a diminishment; the dead speaker does not report on an afterlife of any kind. Nevertheless, the buzz has its own kind of power; it is the last thing that lets the speaker know she is still a part of the living world, even as the fly is a visceral reminder of her death (as others have pointed out, flies are attracted to carrion). The fly simultaneously separates the speaker from and connects her with death. In this way, the ordinary fly becomes the occasion of a moment that is extraordinary in its own right: nothing in the world of the poem is so vivid with movement, color, and sound as the "Blue—uncertain stumbling Buzz." Sound is described as color; the speaker may not be able to "see to see" in her last moment, but the fly allows her to "hear to see." The synesthesia emphasizes the complication and richness of this suspended moment. The fly interposes both for aid *and* for troubling—or perhaps, more accurately, it aids *through* troubling.

Sappho's widely admired Fragment 31 is another example of an interposition that proves both to trouble and to aid its speaker. Here is Anne Carson's translation from *If Not, Winter*:

> He seems to me equal to gods that man
> whoever he is who opposite you
> sits and listens close
> to your sweet speaking
>
> and lovely laughing—oh it
> puts the heart in my chest on wings
> for when I look at you, even a moment, no speaking
> is left in me
>
> no: tongue breaks and thin
> fire is racing under skin
> and in eyes no sight and drumming
> fills ears
>
> and cold sweat holds me and shaking
> grips me all, greener than grass
> I am and dead—or almost
> I seem to me.

Between the speaker and her beloved, to use Dickinson's phrasing, *there interposed a man.*

It is tempting to think that this is a poem about jealously, but as Carson points out in her essay "Ruse" from *Eros the Bittersweet,* Sappho "does not covet the man's place." If she were to change places with the man, "it seems likely she would be entirely destroyed." Carson explains, "It is the beloved's beauty that affects Sappho; the man's presence is somehow necessary to delineation of that emotional event . . . We see in it the radical constitution of desire. For, where eros is lack, its activation calls for three structural components—lover, beloved and that which comes between them . . . The third component plays a paradoxical role for it both connects and separates."

In Carson's translation, when Sappho looks at the beloved for "even a moment," she seems to herself mute, deaf, blind, and almost dead, but when she watches this man who can sit so close, it "puts the heart in [her] chest on wings." The interposed man imposes a distance, a separation between lover and beloved that allows the lover's mind, in the words of Carson, "to construct desire for itself" by considering what all this "seems" to her and thereby to experience eros with enormous intensity: her tongue breaks, fire races under her skin, she shakes in a cold sweat. Sappho is not focused on satisfying her desire but rather on feeling it; it becomes an almost ecstatic experience. She experiences a heightened awareness of her body and her senses, and she also transcends herself. No longer experiencing her body as distinctly her own, she does not say "my tongue," "my skin," "my eyes," "my ears," but simply "tongue," "skin," "eyes," "ears." This is a poem about the experience at hand, not a story about overcoming an obstacle. Whether or not the speaker "gets the girl" is beside the point. Once the dramatic situation has been established, we are not reading for plot or to find out what happens next but to gain intimacy with a thrillingly complex moment of consciousness. In response to the interposed man, the speaker feels differently—or at least, she feels what she was already feeling with more conscious intensity. This is the kind of moment to which poets have long been attuned: an occasion when something intercedes to stop us from seeing, proceeding, or feeling in expected ways.

Another example of something interposing, something getting between a speaker and a beloved, comes from the medieval Welsh poet Dafydd ap Gwilym. Here, from his book *Some Business of Affinity*, is Paul Merchant's translation of Gwilym's "The Mist":

> Yesterday (Thursday, my drinking day)
> was a red-letter mark in the calendar.
> I recovered my faith in women. Worn
> wafer-thin with love, I was invited
> to a love-tryst in the green cathedral,
> a meeting made at my girl's choosing.
>
> No man alive, under blaze of heaven,
> knew of my pact with the shapely girl.
> At sun's rising that Thursday morning
> I leapt from bed brim full of laughter
> and set my course to the small cottage
> where the slim one was expecting me.

But now like a thief on the empty moor
a mist came creeping, a black cortège,
a parchment scroll, rain's manuscript,
clotted curds, a slippery hindrance,
a tin colander starting to rust through,
a fowling net on the swarthy soil.

A dark gate blocking a narrow path,
a winnowing sieve tossed up carelessly,
a monk's grey cowl shading the land,
darkening every vale and hollow,
a thorn fence bestriding the sky,
a purple bruise on the fogbound hill.

It was like wool, a thin veil of fleece
flimsy as smoke, a straw bonnet,
a hedge of rain barring my progress,
a coat of armour, a storm to soak me,
blinding my eyes so I was lost utterly,
a coarse cloak thrown over the county.

Then it was a castle right in my path,
hall of the fairy king, wind's territory,
a pair of fat cheeks chewing the earth,
torchbearers searching a pitchy sky
for its three pallid constellations,
a poet's blindfold, a bard's penalty.

A length of expensive cambric
thrown over the heavens, a halter
of spidery gossamer, French fabric,
on the moorland, fairies' realm,
a filmy breath of piebald smoke,
forest mist on a May morning.

Film on the eyes, a barking kennel,
ointment smeared on Hell's witches,
sodden dew become oddly sinister,
a discarded suit of damp chain-mail.
I'd sooner walk the pitch dark heath
than navigate this mist at noon.

At midnight stars light up the sky,
candles aflame in a dark chancel,
but this morning (bitter memory)
no moon, no stars, only a mist,
a prison door slammed behind me,
this mist, a misery past endurance.

Thus was my path curdled by clouds
leaving a stupefied stone-blind lover
stood stock-still, bereft of the sight
of Morfydd's elegant arching brows.

Once again, it is the something interposed, the something that
gets between, that lends viability to the poem. When the speaker
can no longer physically move forward toward consummation

with his beloved, a space is created in which the imagination runs loose. The language itself becomes a kind of mist: one astonishing metaphor after another comes rushing at us. We feel the speaker's frustration, and the metaphors almost become a series of curses—the mist is a fowling net, a thorn fence, a purple bruise—increasingly comic and absurd. But the more intensely we experience the *presence* of the fog, the more intensely we experience the *absence* of the lover. Because the speaker cannot move toward his beloved's "elegant arching brows," his imagination moves. This is not a poem about mist any more than Sappho's poem is a poem about a man; it is a poem about desire, and it is through the speaker's reaction to the interposing mist that we understand not only the enormity of that desire but also its nature: unsteady, ever shifting. Desire engenders more desire. The not-having energizes the imagination; possibility after possibility unfolds, even in so small a matter as renaming the cursed mist over and over: it is "a halter / of spidery gossamer," "a discarded suit of damp chain-mail." Impeded from his pursuit, this speaker is given the chance to feel the not-having rather than the anticipation of having. Which is to say, he is given a chance to feel.

These three very different poems all feature moments when something (a fly, a man, the fog) is interposed between the speakers and where they have set their sights; the speakers can no longer proceed toward an arrival they have anticipated or desired. Think of the feeling of running and suddenly encountering a gulf or crater or obstacle that you cannot see until you are upon it; it is that sudden sense of imbalance—as you try to steady yourself to keep from falling—that interests these poets. Think of the number of poems that feature speakers who are, as the expression goes, "stopped in their tracks." "The Moose," considered by some to be Elizabeth Bishop's greatest poem, is told from the point of view of a passenger on a bus that is forced to a stop by the tall moose that "looms" in the middle of the road. Standing between the passengers "from narrow provinces / of fish and bread and tea" and their unnamed destination, the moose, "grand, otherworldly," demands their and our attention. The passengers suddenly feel ("[they] all feel") something they haven't felt before on this journey. Similarly, William Stafford's best known poem, "Traveling Through the Dark," unfolds the drama of a speaker who stops his car when he encounters a large animal on the road—a dead deer; however, it is not the deer that turns out to be the interposing object. The unsentimental speaker knows exactly what to do: clear the "heap" so that he and others can pass safely. What stops him—if only momentarily—is the living fetus inside the dead mother. It is this interposed surprise of the fawn, "alive, still, never to be born," that startles the speaker out of the "automatic pilot" response with which he began, startles him into hard thinking, startles him into feeling. An even more famous example is Robert Frost's "Stopping by Woods on a Snowy Evening." Many might overlook the dark woods when passing by them, but they bring Frost's speaker to a full stop. He interrupts his journey, delays his promises, for a loveliness both "dark and deep," and the poem creates that space for us, too.

I believe it is not an accident that so many of the poems I have pointed to are well known to most of us. This kind of dramatic occasion, in which something is interposed between the speaker and his or her destination or desire, seems extraordinarily well suited to poetry. The drama can be staged succinctly: a time, a place, a speaker directed toward something when *something else* gets in the way that provokes an unexpected response.

Please note that I have included no example of a speaker on a stroll who stops to appreciate a particularly striking flower or sunset. None of these speakers sets out with that kind of receptivity; what is interposed is not the thing that the speaker hoped to find. This is key to why these poems are so compelling. Most of us rarely have the quiet and leisure to seek out subjects of contemplation; what hits us where we live is the sense of being in motion, with volition and will, intention and desire, with goals and tasks and "miles to go"—when, unexpectedly, something stops us.

The final poem I want to consider is John Ashbery's "Of Linnets and Dull Time":

> You said you don't want to know any more
> than you do now, of every thing that might be
> a person. It would be cheating. That is urgent.
> If we are going to mean in so many ways
> let them all be lopped off.
> That way we'll know you're getting older.
>
> I feel sorry for anyone that has to die.
> The lines of what's expected
> fan out like beaters. That's all,
> I think. But I lose things, now.
> The beautiful shape of the toilet interposed
> a viability as the air-raid drill ended.
> We've got to do something.

He may be up there now, trying to find us.
If you let me, I'll drive you back to the fairgrounds.

On first read, Ashbery's poem may seem as if he is randomly juxtaposing one thing after another. The beautiful shape of the toilet interposes, but exactly what does it interrupt? Before the toilet, there is the you's desire not to know any more than he already does about the human realm, a resistance to how people mean in multiple ways: "let [the meanings] all be lopped off." There is a drive here—one familiar to many of us—to simplify rather than complicate. Who hasn't wished at times to know less, or at least wished for a break from the ambiguities of human expressions? Wouldn't it be easier if we didn't have to pay attention to implications and possible double meanings of what we and others say?

The first stanza ends with the desire for just one meaning, one point of knowledge. When the second stanza begins, it seems the wished-for simplicity has been granted, but the mood is elegiac: "I feel sorry for anyone that has to die." Here, the poem turns to a focus on loss and what might be lost when meanings are lopped off. This statement is followed by an image of the beaters in a hunting party ready to beat the underbrush to get the prey to come out for the hunters—similar to the way, we imagine, the you would prefer to beat out and kill off any extra meanings of the lines. Then, after four lines focused on scarcity and loss, suddenly "The beautiful shape of the toilet interpose[s] / a viability."

I, for one, find the interposed toilet strangely moving. It is very nearly the opposite of Dickinson's fly. The fly intensifies our awareness of death, of mortality. It comes primarily in the form of sound, ephemeral sound, a buzz the speaker can't hang on to. The toilet, by contrast, is a solid physical entity and has to do with matters that are of exclusive concern to the living. Even those of us mostly stuck in our heads, spending our days primarily with text, must interrupt our reveries with visits to this "beautiful shape." As a concrete object, it stands in contrast to everything else in the poem. Unlike the presence of the you or the world beyond or even the speaker himself, the shape of a toilet is definitive and stable. At first it seems that the toilet might be the ideal of "lopped off" meaning. A toilet is a toilet is a toilet; it doesn't come with a loaded symbolic history. However, as soon as it is made an aesthetic object—it is "beautiful"—how can we not think of Marcel Duchamp's *Fountain*? Of course a toilet can be more than a toilet.

With that, the poem opens up to its most richly ambiguous lines. "We've got to do something" could be read with sincere urgency, as in, "We can't just sit around and be targets. We've got to do something for ourselves. We've got to do something to defy death." Or it could be read with more detachment, as in, "Well, we've got to do something to fill the time. Use the toilet, go to the fairgrounds, et cetera." The next line is equally rich: "He may be up there now, trying to find us." Who is the "he"? God, perhaps. God is the presence most traditionally turned to when death troubles us, when the air-raid sirens go off, and maybe he is not just present and available but actually trying to find us. Then again, maybe the "he" is a pilot coming to drop bombs from the sky; maybe there is a real point to the drills and a real air raid is on its way, the plane up there now, trying to find us. The ambiguity of these lines defies the earlier impulse to "lop off" meaning, an impulse that is linked to diminishment and getting older. The lines defiantly, stridently, mean in many ways. These are the fairgrounds to which Ashbery wants to return us: the realm of play, of vitality, of meaning in many ways. This, Ashbery suggests, is the real realm of the living.

Many poems use techniques of juxtaposition and collage, but my interest here has been in a more specific geometry: something *is interposed between* a speaker and what he or she desires, or something is interposed between a speaker and the destination toward which he or she is moving. A consciousness must face something it did not expect; a consciousness must shift its attention. The speakers exchange forward momentum for suspension: they enter suspended moments in which time slows down and they have the opportunity to reconsider, to see and feel differently.

Of course, the real brilliance in these poems lies in their language: Dafydd's "thorn fence bestriding the sky, / a purple bruise on the fogbound hill"; Dickinson's "Blue—uncertain stumbling Buzz—." I tend to side with Stéphane Mallarmé when he says, "Poetry is the language of a state of crisis." There is a difference between the story of crisis and the language of a state of crisis. Perhaps we would all do well to ask ourselves: Is the language of my poem in service of the story of a crisis? Or is my story in service of the language? These poems offer models of the latter. They deftly and elegantly stage moments of interposition powerful enough to snag a consciousness into a new sense of self, of world, and of language.

STORY & DREAM

JIM KRUSOE

Do you see the story? Do you see anything? It seems to me I am trying to tell you a dream . . . that commingling of absurdity, surprise, and bewilderment in a tremor of struggling revolt, that notion of being captured by the incredible which is the very essence of dreams.

—JOSEPH CONRAD, *Heart of Darkness*

I

MY FIRST CONSIDERATION of the role of dream in fiction began several summers ago, on the Van Wyck Parkway, as my family and I were on our way back from our annual vacation on Long Island. Just as the signs for JFK started to appear, for no perceptible reason at all, my father-in-law, who was driving, began to describe his all-time favorite movie scene.

He said, "I can't remember the actual name of the picture, but Chaplin is in it, and in this movie—whatever it is—he's on the top floor of a skyscraper that's under construction. Suddenly he sees something on the ground that needs his attention, so he jumps onto a construction elevator with a foreman at the controls. The fore-man's back is to Chaplin, and the elevator begins an excruciatingly slow descent. As it drops, inch by inch, and still remains impossibly high above the ground, Chaplin starts to fidget with a coil of hose next to him. First he pulls on it, then he pokes it, until pretty soon he manages to get his finger stuck in the hose's shiny nozzle. He tries to pull his finger out, but it won't budge. He yanks and then the whole hose starts to unroll. The more he struggles, the more it unrolls, until it's wrapped entirely around him."

"That's pretty funny," I said, though I wanted him to pay a little more attention to the road.

"Wait, that's not the best part," my wife's father said, as a brown station wagon with suitcases roped to the top swerved in front of us. "After an eternity, the elevator reaches the ground, and the foreman, who has had his back to Chaplin the whole time, finally turns to see him completely wrapped up in the hose.

"'How did you get yourself into that mess?' the foreman asks.

"Chaplin peers out of the tangled hose as if he's in a jungle and the hose is some kind of a vine. He draws himself up to his full height. 'None of your business,' Chaplin answers."

A dream, I thought to myself. *You've just described a dream.*

Then there was Jet Blue, right in front of us.

Because, come to think of it, it's not so improbable that dreams are the original source of fiction, or at least a co-source, along with memoir. Surely, at one time or another, some caveman, sitting around the fire and bored with the evening's telling about the latest mastodon hunt, must have said to his pals, "Wait a minute. That reminds me of a dream I had the other day . . ." At which point, I'd guess, about half the audience got up and left.

So now let me tell you a real dream I had not long ago. I'll tell it as quickly as possible, because there is nothing like a real dream to make eyes glaze over and strong men leave the room. One morning, just before waking, I dreamed I was test-driving a gleaming-new, black Land Rover, and finding myself at the top of a very steep hill, I looked down and saw that the road had inexplicably turned into an escalator. "Oh well," I said, and began driving the Land Rover onto the escalator, even though I was really worried I might damage the car, but—and here's the point—even as I was driving, a part of me was watching the whole process from the top of the hill, from where I could see the car being successfully driven down the mechanical stairs. When I woke, the peculiarity of this double perspective stayed with me. I wondered how I could be doing two things—watching and driving—at once. And then I thought: in fiction we call this "close third person," and if dreaming has a point of view, it has to be close third.

BUT BEFORE I discuss the similarity of stories and dreams further, let me add a word of caution. Just as being true to life doesn't guarantee good fiction, actual dreams seldom make good stories, because in dreams, the dreamer isn't given a chance to revise, to choose. Stories, however, *do* take place in an area somewhere between dream and life. Patricia Hampl, speaking about painting, reminds us, "A painting must depict the act of seeing, not the object seen." So a work of fiction, like a dream, depicts the act of thinking about the world, not the world.

Let's start with a diagram. You may be familiar with Walter Benjamin's explanation of how commodity—that is, the world of goods—falls between dreams and technology. Although

Benjamin doesn't stress this, goods also represent an agreement reached between sellers and buyers.

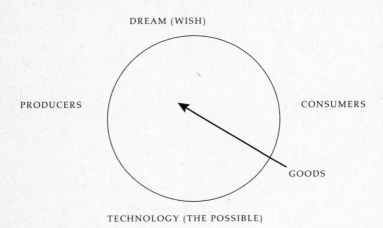

From there it doesn't seem such a very great leap to define the territory of story in a similar fashion:

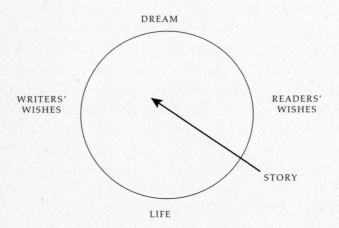

Notice that this diagram is *not* limited to that sort of writing called "dreamy," or "surreal," but encompasses *all* writing, including, and maybe even especially, the most naturalistic. Take the above circle, for example, and then think about what works of fiction would fall inside:

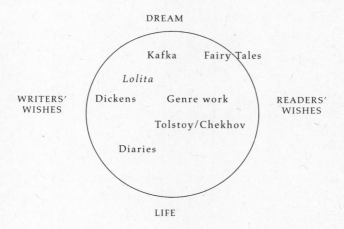

DREAM

Kafka   Fairy Tales

Lolita

WRITERS'   Dickens   Genre work   READERS'
WISHES   WISHES

Tolstoy/Chekhov

Diaries

LIFE

Putting things in their precise place, though, isn't the point. For example, it's entirely plausible that the writer of a genre novel may want exactly the same thing as his or her reader. The point is that, in order to be transmittable, *by definition* stories (including memoirs) have to stay *inside* the circle—although a story (or memoir) can be anywhere at all inside it—to fulfill all four elements. If writing falls outside the circle, then it is merely rhetorical, or random, or pandering, or personal, or a grocery list. It's the tug of all four of these bodies—dream, life, the reader, and the writer—that makes work interesting.

To help explain this concept, let's examine the characteristics of what Freud calls "the dream-work," as he discusses it in *The Interpretation of Dreams*.

The first principle of this work is what Freud calls "condensation." That is, to take a great deal of material and to compress it by means of summary and omission into a manageable form. Of course, a story does the same thing. So it follows that one thing a writer needs to ask about the work is obvious: Can it be said more briefly? Are we guilty of irrelevant information: *She walked across the average-sized room to the heavy, brown, wooden door, where, being right-handed, she cautiously extended her right arm and, opening the shy flower of her hand, firmly grasped the shiny silver doorknob, which protruded from the smooth surface of the wood like a metal . . .* what? Ugh!

And then, wonderfully, as with most maxims, the opposite is also true: Have we given enough time to the really important moments in our story and made them large enough so they can assume their proper weight? *She opened the door. Why was she carrying a snow globe containing a miniature skyscraper amidst slowly falling glitter, and how could she even call a structure smaller than a matchbox a skyscraper? When had she picked it up? She couldn't remember.* (Writing this makes me realize how dream-based fiction is about questions, not answers.)

Speaking of condensing, it's a good idea to check to see if we are repeating ourselves, not only in the reporting of events but also through the multiplication of characters as well. In the course of writing a book, I usually find that I've created at least two or more people who do essentially the same thing, as well as a few too many random walk-ons. In life, we may find ourselves trapped in neurotic repetition, but in fiction and dream, unless the point of the story or the dream *is* the repetition, such repetition usually doesn't move the narrative forward. (The opposite of that truth is that repeated words can create a dream enclosure and signal an inability to escape.)

A dream always begins at exactly the right moment. Life's a mess, but dreams and good stories start, in the words of Michael McClure, "with the spring already compressed." If we think of our story as a dream, it's useful to ask if things are taking too long to begin. Also, when we finish, have we overshot the mark? These questions are fairly standard in writing, but if we read our work as if we had dreamed it, we can see the work more clearly. Dreams, as we know, start in the middle of things and end, well, where they end. Offhand, I can't remember a single dream of mine that ever came with or needed backstory. Nine times out of ten, unless you are Alice Munro and the story *is* the backstory, you can just move on.

The second principle is "displacement." Here again, it seems obvious that a specialty of storytelling, with few exceptions, is to point out how one small act or object can stand in for a larger concept. In fiction, places really *are* sinister, and furniture *does* represent a life (in the real world, interior decorators make a living on this hope). In fiction, a picture of a woman cut from a magazine, her arm buried in a fur muff, can cast a mood over a story about a man who wakes to find he is a beetle. If things were only things in stories (or in life, for that matter), the bowl in Ann Beattie's "Janus" and Henry James's golden bowl someday might appear at a high-class garage sale, along with baby strollers and a wing chair. But in dreams, as in fiction, everything glows from an emission larger than its own. Buddhist nonattachment may be a good rule for getting through the department of motor vehicles, but it has no place in dreams or stories. If the objects in our stories remain only objects, then maybe we are not paying close enough attention.

The third of Freud's principles—that thoughts generally find their expression through "visual images"—is probably the most obviously applicable to story. It's hard to imagine how we can project our interior thoughts if we don't have a stage set, a context, in which to place them. To have a convincing world, a writer must make it unique and distinguish it from the dozens of competing, similar worlds. Dreams do that, and so does fiction, through the use of specific details. If your dreams are like mine, they give the *impression* of possessing a realistic background, but there is really hardly anything at all there, just a few selected details that happen to be the exact ones that are most important to reinforcing and sustaining the illusion. A movie, even the Chaplin one that began this discussion, brings with it a complete backdrop of things near and far, and we can see what every character on screen looks like at every second.

Along these lines, one of my favorite items to come upon in a story is a picture that's described in so much detail that it practically becomes an entire story in itself. The first chapter of José Saramago's *The Gospel According to Jesus Christ*, which describes a painting and nothing else, is among the most moving and beautiful pieces of writing I know. Pictures focus things. The other night I dreamed of my son, Henry, but even as I did, I realized I could recall him only as a collection of moments and expressions, a composite of a real person rather than the individual he is. In other words, I *knew* it was him, but I couldn't really see him. But then, surprisingly and startlingly, resting on a table in the dream was a *photograph* of him—literally his high school photo—in which I could see each detail perfectly. Pictures and photos open out a space like nothing else.

The fourth of Freud's principles is the "treatment of contraries." That is, most dreams contain dramatic opposites, and it's the function of the dream to reconcile them. If a story doesn't have a figure in opposition to the main figure, perhaps you can add one, not only to create a more complete, and therefore more real, world but also to bring out the unique qualities of a main character. Once, for example, I had a dream in which Richard Nixon had started a literary magazine and was about to use one of my stories, but had asked for a few changes. Someone, maybe Goethe, wrote that good and evil are both sides of the same coin. If we are creating real fictions, then both positive and negative qualities should always be present in individual characters and in our palette of characters.

To the above let me add a few more attributes of dreams, also taken from Freud, that may be helpful in the business of storytelling. First, every dream must have a hero, a main character with whom the dreamer identifies, but who is *not* under the dreamer's control (if he were, why would we watch him or her?). I'm not saying every single story absolutely *has* to have a central character, but if a story doesn't, it should be on purpose, not just because we forgot to create one or haven't decided who it's to be.

Freud quotes the psychologist Gustav Fechner, who describes his own dreams by saying, "It is as if the psychological activity were transferred from the brain of a reasonable being into the brain of a fool." Or, in the words of Emerson, "Dreams retain the infirmities of our characters." And of course, though Emerson meant our *moral* characters, it works perfectly for fictional ones as well. Sad to say, but upstanding, wise, tasteful people do not make for a good story. Oedipus is remembered for being wrong, and in James's *The Portrait of a Lady*, it's not Isabel Archer's right choices that make her great, but the fact that she misjudges both her power and Gilbert Osmond. (Notice how names are always important in James, as they are in dreams.) If you want to create a believable character, for God's sake, don't make him perfect. It seems to me more than coincidence that the German word for dream, *traum*, is based on the same Greek root for "wound" as the English word *trauma*. Maybe we dream to heal a wound. Or just to find one.

Freud devoted an entire monograph to the uncanny, which he defines as a sensation in part familiar and in part not. The equivalent, though less exciting, term we use in fiction is "defamiliarization." That is, when things are as expected, a reader doesn't have to pay attention. When something is not quite familiar, readers will watch it more closely. (The third extreme—when things are completely strange—will cause some readers to look more intently, won't even register with others, or will make others so uncomfortable they'll just quit.)

Remember that in a dream we don't know what the outcome will be. In fiction too, with exceptions, it's best that the ending arrives not as a result of premeditation but flows from the events that precede it. Someone, maybe Hemingway and maybe Doctorow—the line has been attributed to both—once said that a writer should only be able to look a little distance ahead, as if he were driving late at night and his vision was limited to the reach of his headlights. This limited vision forces both writers and readers to pay attention. Likewise, though a writer will have partial control over his or her characters, it should never be complete. For writers, the metaphor of Frankenstein's monster is a happy one: our brain in someone else's body. Or maybe the reverse.

In a dream, as well, there is usually a heightened sense of risk, or at least of significance. I may have a pointless dream, even a lot of them, but while I'm sleeping, every act seems important and has my complete attention.

II

THERE ARE OTHER useful benefits that come from linking the writing process with the dreaming one. Most stories I can think of, when broken down, seem really just types of dreams (with novels being a series of dream sequences). Therefore, when a story, or even a scene we are trying to write, stalls, it may be because we have abandoned dream-logic in favor of expediency and/or dull reality. Consider the following list of dream scripts, and then imagine them as stories you've read, or written, or might someday write:

Arriving somewhere unprepared
Arriving without clothes, or with an important object missing
Having done a horrible thing and worrying people will find out
People accusing you falsely

People accusing you justly
Flying (that is, doing something that by all rights should be
    impossible)
Being pursued
Going to a strange town
Meeting an unusual person
Shape-shifting
Being invisible
Being in a place where things don't work
Rage
Anxiety
Powerlessness
Inexplicable sexual attraction
Being dead and watching what is happening
Trying to find something
Committing a criminal act
Witnessing a criminal act by someone else
Finding a mysterious object

And in fact, if we view a few familiar stories through the dream lens, we may be surprised by how many resemble dreams: The opening of *Great Expectations* has a boy seized by a strange and threatening figure who rises out of a marsh and forces him to do something against his will. *Moby-Dick* begins with Ishmael getting on a boat that people warn him not to board, a boat named the *Pequod*—a name right out of a dream—and at the close of the novel, the sailors row after Moby Dick even as their oars are being reduced to splinters by sharks, and a bird is nailed by its wing to the mast of the sinking ship. Talk about dream images! In Kafka's "A Hunger Artist" (and also, in a way, in *The Metamorphosis*), a man becomes invisible. In Chekhov's "The Lady with a Pet Dog," a man meets a mysterious woman, has sex, she disappears, and he finds her again. In James's "The Beast in the Jungle," something very important is about to happen, but never does.

More contemporarily, in Richard Ford's "Rock Springs" a man traveling across the country in a stolen car with his daughter and his girlfriend breaks down in the middle of the night. He gets out, leaving his daughter and girlfriend in the car, and walks to where he sees a light on in the distance. It is a trailer occupied by an old black woman; they have a conversation about gold. He leaves, a stranger gives him a ride, and the story ends with him alone in the middle of a motel parking lot. In Mary Gaitskill's "A Romantic Weekend," two sexually charged, and apparently compatible, lovers try to get together, but nothing goes right.

And so on, without even mentioning Borges, or Poe, Flannery O'Connor, or those writers, like Hawthorne in "Young Goodman Brown," who address the act of dreaming directly. "For a long time I used to go to bed early," Proust begins his great novel. And I think: *in order to dream.*

Also, if we use a dream model for narration, a story is freed (if we want it to be) from the usual story arc with the rising action bunched together in the middle. With this dream model, there can be any range of action, from a lot to none, or several actions, because a story's significance is its meaning, not just its action, and a good story, like a good dream, will shadow us the rest of the day. In fact, it will shadow us as long as we wish, and that is one of the great and secret pleasures of rewriting. In the process of adjusting a story to what it needs to be, each time we rewrite we are able to reenter the dream. We read, we change this and that, and then there we are; we are in it.

So the point here is simple and entirely opportunistic: if we can give our narrative the power of a dream, whether the narrative is naturalistic, or even autobiographical, its power will be enriched in ways that are entirely different than when we begin and remain in the dreary realm of familiar narrative sequence— that is, the ordinary that occupies most of our days.

Sometimes it seems to me that the unstated goal of all writing workshops is to try to formulate some set of always-elusive rules for success, but even as I make them up for myself and others, it's important to remember that it's a lost cause. The minute we start having *rules*, especially ones that are supposed to access the unconscious, the more we try to outguess the creative process, which is as old as . . . well . . . dreaming. Remember that great fable about the shoemaker and the elves, in which every morning the shoemaker wakes to find that his shoes have been finished while he slept. (This action also takes place in a workshop!) The minute the shoemaker attempts to spy on the process, trying to discover the secret, the elves leave him, never to return. "None of your business," they say.

As writers, our work is to create dreams that others can experience with the same intensity and vividness. The more I write, the more I've come to believe in the primacy of dream and story. That is to say, I believe it is our stories, even more than our memories, that define who we are. So who is more real, to paraphrase Borges, the Me in my dreams or the one in my stories?

I don't know if it matters, only that they both be present.

DO SOMETHING

CHRISTOPHER R. BEHA

WHEN I STARTED writing seriously—by which I mean that I was serious in my intentions and commitment, which seem to me the main things a writer can control—I started by writing sentences. I spent a lot of time, sometimes a day, sometimes the better part of a week, on each one, moving its parts around, weighing the thing in my hand, struggling to achieve balance and shapeliness, waiting for all the pieces to click perfectly into place.

Paul Valéry once told André Breton that he couldn't be a novelist because he refused to write, "The Marquise went out at five o'clock." Fiction writing, Breton and Valéry agreed, relies too much on sentences written in this "purely informative style," sentences of a "circumstantial, needlessly specific nature"—why five o'clock? why not five thirty? and why not a princess? In those early days of writing, I thought often of Valéry's remark. I wanted to write fiction, but I didn't want to write that kind of bluntly functional sentence. I wanted each sentence to be a thing unto itself, sufficient and entire. Needless to say, these sentences were all a long way from "The Marquise went out at five o'clock."

Each sentence necessarily represented an end point, since it's precisely the nature of sufficient things that they don't have needs that must be met beyond their own borders. They don't make demands that bring new things into existence. So I always felt, after finishing one, that I was starting from scratch. Naturally, I'd write another sentence, but it wouldn't bear any relationship to the one I'd just completed. Again, necessarily so: sufficient things don't have relationships.

This was in college, when I was taking writing workshops. What would happen is that I would go on in this way awhile, until I had perhaps a dozen such sentences. It would then occur to me that I had to turn them into a piece that I could submit to class, so I'd lay my sentences out and write a bunch more to connect them into something that could reasonably be called a story. These connective sentences were written much more quickly, with far less care.

If this doesn't sound like a very good way to go about writing stories, it isn't. And the stories I wrote in this way weren't very good. This was as obvious to me as it was to anyone who was forced to read them. But things weren't completely hopeless: my professors and classmates sometimes picked out isolated sentences that they believed contained enough life and interest to suggest some promise on my part. You may have already guessed that the sentences they picked were never—I'm not exaggerating: not once—those I'd labored over.

There was obviously a lesson to be had here, but I wasn't sure what it was. For a while, I thought it had to do with spontaneity.

The sentences I'd spent all my time on felt mannered, uptight. The sentences I'd written quickly had a breezy vitality. I tried to write entirely in this breezy way, but I couldn't do it without already having those more carefully constructed sentences—the "real" sentences—to link up. And I couldn't trick myself into writing my "real" sentences like throwaways, though I experimented with various approaches to get over this barrier. On the advice of one teacher, I tried "free" writing—first thought, best thought. On the advice of another, I attempted self-hypnosis. On my own initiative, I drank before sitting down to work. In all cases the results were a mess.

Eventually, I just went back to laboring. I decided I had to work harder, but that part of my work would be making the writing feel *less* worked over. I thought of it as the literary equivalent of stonewashing jeans or building with distressed wood—creating pleasing imperfections by first polishing and then artfully tarnishing. I built an entire novel this way. It took me a long time to do it, and the novel wasn't any good.

This might have gone on much longer than it did except that, while working on that novel, I began writing nonfiction. Mostly I wrote book reviews, but also some essays and long-form journalism. After I'd finished the novel that wasn't very good, I wrote a memoir. Among other things, this memoir was about the illness and death of a person I loved. When writing all this nonfiction, I labored over my sentences, but it was a different kind of labor. If you write about actual people and you are a halfway responsible human being, the mandate to account accurately for your subject is going to take precedence over everything else. So I spent a lot of time on my sentences, but I did so with a greater end in mind, which was making sure that those sentences captured the truth as I understood it. The results were better than anything I'd written before, and better than the fiction I was writing at the same time.

Once again there was a lesson to be had, and once again I didn't know what it was. If the lesson was that I wrote better when I felt an obligation to the truth, I wasn't sure how to apply it to my fiction writing, which was the writing that mattered most to me. More than one person suggested that the lesson was that I simply wasn't a very good fiction writer, that I should be grateful that I could write nonfiction that people would pay to read, which put me ahead of most aspiring writers, and that I should stop driving myself crazy doing something for which I had no demonstrable talent. That wasn't a lesson I was willing to accept. I was going to write fiction no matter what, so I might as well try to figure out how to do it properly. In fact, even knowing that the novel I'd spent six years on wasn't any good, as I finished my memoir, I was mapping out a new novel in my head.

When you map a book out in your head, you don't build it with sentences, since you can't fit that many sentences in your head at once. You build it with images or scenes. Or you lay out the structure, or you outline the plot. I do some combination of all these things. In any case, the very day I sent my publisher the final changes to my memoir, I started writing what would become my first published novel. By then, the book already existed in some inchoate form in my head, and my job was to get it onto the page. There wasn't the same kind of moral imperative that comes with nonfiction: I'd made everything up, so I didn't owe it to anyone other than myself to render it truthfully, and I made

changes to the initial conception whenever they seemed justi-
fied, many of them quite substantial. But I had finally learned
the lesson, and it applied to my fiction as well as my nonfiction:
Whenever my sentences had a function outside themselves—
whether that function was connecting up other sentences, hon-
oring the truth of a loved one's life, or setting down an imagined
world already existent in my head—they could in time be made
to work. Whenever my sentences were built to be beautiful yet
self-sufficient objects of attention, they collapsed.

IT'S LONG BEEN my experience that after I learn a valuable
lesson through a lengthy and costly period of trial and error, I will
find that lesson stated in the most explicit terms in all sorts of
places where I might easily have found it before. So I should not
have been surprised, while I was working on the second novel, to
come across the following passage in one of my favorite books:

> These things I then knew not, and I loved these lower beauties,
> and I was sinking to the very depths, and to my friends I said,
> "Do we love any thing but the beautiful? What then is the
> beautiful? and what is beauty? What is it that attracts and wins
> us to the things we love? for unless there were in them a grace
> and beauty, they could by no means draw us unto them." And
> I marked and perceived that in bodies themselves, there was a
> beauty, from their forming a sort of whole, and again, another
> from apt and mutual correspondence, as of a part of the body
> with its whole, or a shoe with a foot, and the like. And this
> consideration sprang up in my mind, out of my inmost heart,
> and I wrote "on the fair and fit," I think, two or three books.

This comes from Augustine's *Confessions*. It's a minor passage—the actual volumes Augustine wrote "on the fair and fit" have been lost—but I couldn't believe I'd taken so little notice of it in the half dozen previous times I'd read the book. Augustine is describing precisely the distinction I'd been failing to make all that time: there is a beauty to be found in a well-made whole, a body itself; then there is the beauty of a part in the whole, which is the beauty of a thing that elegantly serves its purpose. When it comes to writing stories or novels, sentences are parts, not wholes. They need to be both fair *and* fit. They can't be treated as bodies themselves.

Finally, it's not a limitation but a virtue of the novel that it demands its author to write, "The Marquise went out at five o'clock." Within the context of the novel, such a sentence can even be beautiful, because it can be made necessary. This is the truth that another poet, W. H. Auden, gets at when he says that the novelist

> Must struggle out of his boyish gift and learn
> How to be plain and awkward, how to be
> One after whom none think it worth to turn
>
> . . . .
> Become the whole of boredom, subject to
> Vulgar complaints like love, among the Just
>
> Be just, among the Filthy filthy too.

Another bit of advice I'd read half a dozen times and didn't understand until I'd learned it in my own way.

People can disagree, and have, over whether a novel or a story must itself have a "purpose" apart from being beautiful. But it seems to me inarguable that the parts of a novel or a story must have a purpose within the whole. These days, when I find that a sentence I'm writing isn't working, I don't think about what I want that sentence to look like or to be; I don't pull it from the page to weigh it in my hand; I don't worry over its internal balance. I simply ask myself, "What do I need this sentence to *do*?" I ask myself what role the sentence plays in its paragraph, what role the paragraph plays in its scene, the scene in its story. If I can't answer these questions, even in some inarticulate and intuitive way, then I've got a problem, and that problem is bigger than this one sentence.

IF THIS BIT of hard-won knowledge sounds fairly obvious, I can only say in my defense that nothing about the academic creative writing complex as I experienced it encourages this attitude. The problem goes as deep as the very name of the discipline. I suspect that the perpetual debate about whether "creative writing" can be taught would cease if we just had a moratorium on that unfortunate moniker. No good teacher thinks that creativity can be taught; no good teacher doubts that writing—in the sense of a set of tools with which a writer can tackle literary problems—can be. Yet how often are beginning writing students who are not yet up to putting together an entire story placed in front of an object and asked to describe it in writing, in the way that students of painting and drawing are asked to render still lifes or the human form? Instead, they are simply told to write something that is in turn given to other students who are asked to judge it without any reference to what the piece of writing is supposed to be doing, what part it might play in a larger whole. The result, I suspect, is lots of students doing as I did, tirelessly perfecting sentences that serve no purpose, forever chasing the fair without ever considering the fit.

My own experience as a teacher has been that students are initially resistant to writing exercises, which they see as an infringement upon their self-expression. They are likely to be impatient if you suggest that these exercises will actually give them the tools necessary for self-expression, let alone that great writing might not even have that much to do with self-expression, in the end. But if you push them on it, if you set them to specific tasks, they will see improvement almost immediately and thus be encouraged to persist. I have had students admit to a great feeling of relief at being given an assignment at which they could succeed because even though they were certain that they wanted to write, they didn't yet know *what* they wanted to write, and learning both the how and the what of writing at once is an overwhelming task.

There is another way that creative writing workshops at almost every level contradict the functional view I'm proposing. In most creative writing workshops, you will be encouraged to write short stories, even if your ambition is simply to write novels. (Once you've "graduated" from workshops, of course, you will be encouraged to write novels, even if your ambition is simply to write short stories, but this is another matter.) The idea is that stories are easier in some way, if not to write, then to discuss in class. But if it's true that sentences and paragraphs need to be judged as parts of a whole, then it follows that the sentences and paragraphs of a short story—which is quite obviously a dramatically different form from the novel—need to be judged on different terms than the sentences and paragraphs of a novel. Treating short story writing as preparation for novel writing suggests that a good sentence is a good sentence, irrespective of its fitness to a particular task.

HERE IS WHAT I'm not saying: I'm not saying that writing ought to be transparent, that language that draws attention to itself is an extravagance. I'm certainly not saying that a novelist must have a "purely informative style." Nor am I saying that style should be of only secondary concern. In fact, I still more or less think that style is everything. But style, as Proust said, is just a way of looking at the world. It emerges from the effort to express something other than itself. You don't develop a style by writing sentences that have no purpose other than to be stylish, sentences that seek to be self-contained works of art.

Admittedly, some truly great novelists, like Joyce and Flaubert and Nabokov, went a long way with the belief that every sentence should be a work of art. To this observation I have two responses. First, if you have the talent of Joyce or Flaubert or Nabokov, you should immediately cease listening to anything I have to say about writing. But second, if we're being honest, even Joyce and Flaubert and Nabokov were in their ways harmed by this belief, achieved what they did more in spite of than because of it, and did their worst work when they were most committed to it.

Finally, the advice to make your sentences do something doesn't rest on a particular attitude about the function of literature. It applies equally to traditionalists and experimentalists, to realists and to metafictionists. In a way, it doesn't matter *what* you ask your sentences to do, as long as you ask them to do something. But my own experience has taught me that sentences have the best chance to fit their purpose elegantly when the work they're being asked to do is fairly modest. One of the biggest surprises of my writing life so far has been the questions that occupy my thoughts when I'm writing. When reading great literature—the kind that made me want to write in the first place—I ask questions like "What is my attitude toward death?" or "How can meaning persist in the absence of God?" Because I want readers of my own work to be provoked into asking similar questions, I had long assumed that writing would involve my spending a lot of time on them. But when I write I am occupied by narrow questions specific to the work at hand, like "How do I get from this scene to that scene?" or "How do I make this character's frustrations clear?"

If I'm lucky, my answers to these questions will implicitly suggest a relationship to all the persistent questions that I want my writing "really" to be about. I think this is what Annie Dillard means when she says that a writer must aim for the chopping block and not for the wood. But in the meantime, one advantage to the more modest questions is that they have answers. Those answers may not always be easy to find, but I long ago moved past the idea that the solution to my problems is to work *less* hard. At the very least, finding the perfect answer to a simple question seems feasible enough to get me started, to get me doing something.

ENGINEERING IMPOSSIBLE ARCHITECTURES

KAREN RUSSELL

I. "So Real That It Is Fantastic"

As a kid growing up in Miami, I lived in the closet of my mind, trying on costumes. Later, I'd go to college and read textbooks in which academics try to shove the universe into various corsets, but as a kid, I wasn't reading for that kind of knowledge, that kind of adult girdle or belt. I just wanted to wear new skins. I wanted scales and wings. I'd figured out that you could do these really bizarre tricks in the library, in full view of the imperturbably cheerful librarians. You could, for example, metamorphose. You could suture a character's wings to your eight-year-old body. You could drop time like a skirt and step outside its wrinkled orbit. In the span of one hour on a rainy, ordinary Wednesday, you could live several lifetimes; commune with the dead; kill a man, without remorse, in the Western Territories; run off with traveling carnivals; fall in and out of love; or fall down a rabbit hole in your backyard and land in another galaxy. (This last thing was always happening to British kids in the YA novels I liked; I think those Brits need better zoning laws.) I dutifully checked out Brontë novels to throw the teachers off my scent, but inside my desk I had a stash of fairy tales and science fiction—Jack London, Ray Bradbury, Madeleine L'Engle, Stephen King, Frank Herbert. The skins I got to wear when reading these books were thick hibernation whites, electronic carapaces, martian plumage, whole-body carnival tattoos, the black straitjackets of nightmares—these skins were not restrictive; they were great traveling clothes. All of my favorite voyages as a young reader occurred inside of them.

In the Miami-Dade public library system, if a book was identified as HORROR/FANTASY/SCI-FI, it got quarantined behind the beanbag chairs and labeled with a sticker of a cross-eyed dragon. A fat dragon in bad need of an optometrist—this was how I came to think of myself, as a consumer of fantasy and horror books. I developed the false ideas that, first, there was some essential division between the kinds of books I best loved and "Literature/Fiction" and, second, that there was something deeply suspect about the absorbing pleasure of "genre." *Anna Karenina, The Great Gatsby*—these were the books to emulate. *Dune* and *Cujo* I zipped into my bag and when caught out with such books, would deny what I was doing with the confident cowardice of Peter in the Bible. (Cool guy: "So, you're reading *The Mirror of Her Dreams*, huh?" Me, peering over the spine of *The Mirror of Her Dreams*: "No.")

When I took my first creative writing class, I wrote many stillborn stories about matters pertaining to the "real" world: adultery and dinner parties; zero dragons. If my favorite traveling outfits as a young reader had been rabbit fur and jaundiced Frankenstein skin, now I wore nude panty hose and sensible pumps. But, paradoxically, the more I tried to portray the "real" world, to whip married adults into plausible dramas and describe the makes and models of their cars, the more these stories felt like a stiff, self-conscious ventriloquy of reality. These Raymond Carver–wannabes were boring and grim, and a betrayal of my actual emotional experience of the world. "Flat cola stories," I came to think of them. I was trying so hard to get the facts right that these stories lacked any effervescent sense of creation, discovery, something bubbling under the surface.

Then a favorite professor of mine turned me on to several wild authors, some of whom will be discussed later in this essay—Kevin Brockmeier, George Saunders, Kelly Link, Italo Calvino—world-class literary stylists whose sentences sing, whose characters have integrity and complexity (even when they are young children or ghosts or dinosaurs). Here were writers of serious adult literature drawing upon the oneiric power of fairy tales and fables. Borrowing the technique of uncanny estrangement from horror and science fiction. Handing monsters the mic and letting them crack jokes. I was awed by their ability to demolish the "real" world of a midwestern Tuesday and rearrange the rubble into something glowing and new. Out of the dynamited materials of the everyday, these authors had engineered impossible architectures: escalators to the underworld, moon ladders. They extended my notion of what literature can be and do. They gave me permission to write in twilight, at midnight, on islands, in much weirder and blurrier seasons. I saw that these sorts of genre-bending stories aren't mere kid's stuff, not at all. They have an extraordinary power: to draw out the deep strangeness of what we too often dismiss as "the everyday."

In *Philosophical Investigations*, Wittgenstein writes, "The aspects of things that are most important for us are hidden because of their simplicity and familiarity. (One is unable to notice something—because it is always before one's eyes.)" What I loved about these writers was the way they gave me new goggles with which to consider the "known" world. After observing how characters respond to the altered universes of Kelly Link and Kevin Brockmeier (a haunted mansion in North Carolina, say, or a city where sores and wounds emit light), I'd return to my own world with keener eyesight, a fresh appreciation for the mysterious properties of "the ordinary." I'd put the book down and blink my way back into my bedroom as if for the first time.

None of this is meant as a knock on "realist" fiction (if such a thing exists!). Turning a seed packet of words into a permanent landscape inside a reader's mind is an eerie accomplishment, whether that setting is a Ray Bradbury moon colony or Stuart Dybek's Chicago. But let's say, for the purpose of this essay, that you, too, are interested in engineering an impossible architecture in your fiction, a place that does not exist on any of our school globes or gas station atlases—a world like Macondo, or Narnia, or the spider-web city of Octavia. How does one begin?

In her essay "Writing Short Stories," Flannery O'Connor says:

Fiction is an art that calls for the strictest attention to the real—whether the writer is writing a naturalistic story or a fantasy. I mean that we always begin with what is or what has an eminent possibility of truth about it. Even when one writes a fantasy, reality is the proper basis of it. A thing is fantastic because it is so real, so real that it is fantastic . . . I would even go so far as to say that *the person writing a fantasy has to be even more strictly attentive to the concrete detail than someone writing in a naturalistic vein*—because the greater the story's strain on the credulity, the more convincing the properties in it have to be. (italics added)

That's the challenge, no matter what kind of fiction you are writing: to convince the reader, through the art of detail, that the story you are telling is a true one.

In other words, no matter how whacked-out or strange or funny or (fill in the blank) your setting turns out to be, no reader will be able to live there for long unless it also feels solid enough to support a genuine emotional connection.

II. The Kansas:Oz Ratio

SOME OF THE most successful fantasies I've read take a matter-of-fact approach to even their strangest events. Characters don't "protest too much" or apologize for the crazy thing in their fiction (a chimpanzee narrator, an undersea setting) through compulsive exposition/explanation. The apocalyptic plague called "The Blinks" in Kevin Brockmeier's fabulous *The Brief History of the Dead*; Gregor Samsa's rebirth as that big bug in *The Metamorphosis*; the specter that floats placidly over the fields in Chekhov's "The Black Monk"—all of these supernatural/impossible occurrences are narrated in a naturalistic vein, *as if real*. Which is to say, they are presented to the reader with the same attention to detail as the story's more banal elements: the grain of a wooden desk, the sound of frogs croaking, the red of sunset. A ghost and a pen nib are painted with the same deft brushstrokes.

In "The Black Monk," for example, Chekhov's protagonist, Kovrin, describes the monk, a mirage that appears as a black dervish, with the same steady tone and precise language that he uses for milk and moustaches and tree roots. The story details a vacation to the Russian countryside, and not one of its events deviates from our expectations about the laws that govern reality until one scene about halfway in: Kovrin is standing in "a wide field covered with young rye not yet in blossom," admiring the sunset, "the evening glow . . . flaming in immensity and splendor." Suddenly, "a monk, dressed in black, with a grey head and black eyebrows" comes floating toward him over the rye. Kovrin "move[s] aside into the rye to make way for it, and only just ha[s] time to do so" before the monk "vanishe[s] like smoke."

Everything in this scene, from the unripe rye to the monk's black eyebrows, is related to the reader with the same vivid detail through Kovrin's wondering eyes. What's always impressed me is the detail about how Kovrin moves out of the monk's way—that's the gesture that convinces me that the monk has a definite, albeit uncanny, reality for Kovrin. His involuntary reaction to a wondrous event gives this scene its "eminent possibility of truth." Like Kovrin, I am ducking out of the phantom's way, watching slack-jawed as it dissolves into the trees. Reader and character merge in this vertiginous moment—because Kovrin's reaction to the eerie manifestation is our own. Rooted in the rye fields, well grounded in the story's concrete reality, we are also encouraged by Chekhov to abandon the known world and soar. Kovrin's very human reaction to the apparition (bewilderment, exhilaration, instinctive recoil) gives the phantasmagoric scene the texture of a memory. A supernatural event, told in the "naturalistic vein," becomes believable and affecting.

One nice result of this approach—consistency of tone/precision of detail, no matter what is being described—is that our prejudices about what is fantastic and what is banal start to break down; *everything* begins to feel strange and wondrous. We are cured of the blindness that Wittgenstein cites, our inability to sense the mystery in the "everyday," and soon the Russian sunset seems every bit as fantastic as the Black Monk.

Marianne Moore once famously said that she thinks that poets are "literalists of the imagination" and that a poem should be "an imaginary garden with a real toad in it."

I'm currently working on a novel set during the Dust Bowl, and one of the narrators is a talking scarecrow. I feel as if I am taking a *real* garden—the historical reality of the Dust Bowl—and inserting an imaginary toad—this nattering old, pseudo-magical scarecrow—into it. So my interest in this question of "naturalistic" vs. fantastic/otherworldly/magical detail comes directly from my own struggle to engineer an impossible architecture. What kinds of concrete details, exactly, are required? How do you mix the right sort of otherworldly cement? I've started to think of this as the Kansas:Oz ratio; you could just as easily call it the Supernatural:Natural ratio, or the Timeless/Mythic:Historic/Linear ratio, or the Batshit-Insane Stuff:Banal Tuesday ratio. Real Toads:Imaginary Gardens.

Kansas:Oz is my way to think about the vibrational feedback generated by juxtaposing fantastic and realistic details in a story or novel. Unsettling echoes can result from their interaction. These details can mutually confirm one another (e.g., both Gregor Samsa's exoskeleton and the bedposts are made out of solid material), even as, on another level, their interplay causes the earth beneath a reader to tremble and suggests that our whole idea of "reality" might be a slippery, glorious fiction. This is the central instability exploited by the writer of a fantasy: if Oz is given solid life, through concrete detail, then Kansas can begin to feel dream-like and fragile. Certain bedrock truths that we take for granted in our "everyday" are loosened, spaded up, and reexamined.

But before any of this exciting, seismic stuff can happen, you've got this big challenge: How do you convince a reader to go along with you for the ride? What kind of grit, grain, and mortar from Kansas do you need to import into your Oz to ground your readers, to inspire their confidence in your narrator's voice? How can you use concrete details to earn the right to do something truly crazy on the page and have it believed?

I'll return to my own experience for an example, since I can't vouch for whatever entomological research Kafka did to write *The Metamorphosis*. (Though, my guess is: none. So maybe the lesson there is, if you're Kafka, ignore everything I'm telling you.)

To earn the authority to present a scarecrow as a viable character to readers, I felt I needed to acquire a deep knowledge of the history of the Dust Bowl—a familiarity with the soil in which he is, literally, staked. I wanted to import lumber from the real world to build a universe around the scarecrow, so I read up on suitcase farmers; crop tables; the Farm Security Administration; and Black Sunday—a dust storm that buried houses and cars, electrocuted watermelons, and erased the sun for hours. (You can see where the line between reality and fantasy begins to dilate and blur.) Mad creations work best when assembled out of the terrestrial, out of the dirt of the author's and the readers' lived experience. Any dream Oz that we construct derives its color and its meaning through its analogy to our readers' "ordinary" lives. Magical-realist worlds, in fact, could be thought of as "scrambled Kansases." O'Connor points out:

> If we admit, as we must, that appearance is not the same thing as reality then we must give the artist the liberty to make certain rearrangements of nature if these will lead to greater depths of vision. The artist himself always has to remember that what he is rearranging *is* nature, and that he has to know it and be able to describe it accurately in order to have the authority to rearrange it at all.

III. Follow Your Yellow-Brick Road to a Consistent, Rule-Governed Dream World

ONE LESSON THAT I have to relearn continually is that writing fiction set in an alternate reality doesn't mean you get a free pass to do any crazy thing you want. If you're going to try a Kansas:Oz shuffle, a radical "rearrangement of nature," you have some additional responsibilities to the reader. Namely, that you don't get tripped out on your godlike power (or more likely just exhausted and forgetful) and violate the parameters of the world that you've created.

Many of my early stories failed to create a consistent, rule-governed world, an Oz of sturdy emerald construction. They took place in frictionless worlds where I myself felt like a tourist with only a shallow sense of the laws and customs, places where anything was possible and there was no discernible center of gravity. I kept changing the rules as I was going, so the stakes were nonexistent—it was a world that wasn't governed, that wasn't consistent, so nothing was at stake. It wasn't a world of consequences, so readers didn't care what happened.

As difficult as it is to get a reader to suspend disbelief, it's even harder to keep his or her disbelief lofted over the course of a story or novel as it progresses. In the same way that you can break a reader's heart by playing fast and loose with the rules of your Oz, you can also fail a reader by getting sloppy on the Kansas details. Here's my own embarrassing cautionary tale: I recently got proofs back for my first novel, *Swamplandia!* In one chapter, Ava, the female protagonist, hatches out of a glowing red alligator in a reptile incubator in the Florida swamp. A few pages later, I had written that she falls out of "a forty-foot tree." The copy editor gave me a pass on the red dragon, but that forty-foot-tall tree was circled three times. She'd attacked it with editorial lightning bolts. Her note read: "Is this a joke or a mistake?"

So the red dragon was okay, but I had to do a panicked, humiliated revision to the forty-foot tree.

I think this is a good lesson about the danger of imprecise details. Somehow, a mutant, strawberry-red lizard was more plausible in the world I'd created than a child's forty-foot fall. Why? My guess is that a reader's belief in the red alligator is predicated on Ava's own reaction to it—she finds the gator "miraculous," just as we might, but she goes on to assure us that it is real; it needs food and water like any hatchling gator; in other words, it obeys certain natural laws we recognize. Its blinking eyes and scales are described by Ava in the same straightforward register she would use to describe an ice-cream cone or her sister's hair color. To Ava, and hopefully to the generous reader, the red alligator is a strange-yet-true entity. In contrast, when Ava falls out of that "forty-foot" tree, she doesn't call her survival "miraculous," doesn't check for a broken femur or anything; she just dusts off her swamp culottes and continues rambling on about her sister. That concrete detail, "forty-foot," was my own lazy mistake. So, because I had not earlier indicated that Ava had an adamantine skeleton, and because gravity still seems to operate in the Florida swamps of this novel exactly as it does for us tumblers out here in the "real" world, readers were guaranteed to be confused and distracted by my Kansas detail gone awry. The copy editor's faith in Ava's narration, and in the entire cosmos of the novel, was rattled.

This is what I mean by "a consistent, rule-governed world." In the kind of Kansas:Oz ratio I'd set up in *Swamplandia!*, no way should a kid fall a fatal distance, get up, and walk away like a cat on its ninth life. There should be a serious consequence (911, broken bones) or, at any rate, some kind of acknowledgement within the text of the story that a law has just been violated. When my characters weren't jarred by a forty-foot fall, my readers were.

IV. The Interior World of Oz

I'VE SPENT A lot of time discussing "the concrete detail" and its ability to pin down the reality of both Kansas and Oz for a reader. I would add that a person writing a fantasy must also be strictly attentive to *emotional* detail. As I mentioned above, I missed the boat on a concrete detail, flubbing the realistic height of a tree; but just as crucially, I also failed to give Ava a credible human reaction to her fall. You need concrete detail to establish the bricks-and-mortar reality of your alternate world: its fauna and truck stops and weather. But equally vital, I think, is the convincing emotional detail. Characters must have convincingly human reactions to their world for it to feel real.

Sometimes the details that fully convince me of a twilight zone aren't descriptions of the setting itself, per se; they are details that reveal the private, emotional worlds of the characters who occupy it. In Kevin Brockmeier's *The Brief History of the Dead*, millions have been killed by a lethal virus unleashed by the Coca-Cola Company. (And there's a Kansas detail for you—Coca-Cola—to confirm the fictive, apocalyptic plague!) All of the newly dead are reincarnated in a purgatorial zone they call "The City," which looks a little like Main Street, USA, where they continue to exist as long as someone alive on earth still remembers them. A brilliant, wild premise that becomes absolutely plausible as soon as you hear "eyewitness testimony" from credible sources like the character Jeremy Fallon: "Jeremy Fallon, sixteen, and from Park Falls, Wisconsin"—those are some pretty Kansas details, right?—"said that the fighting hadn't spread in from the coasts yet, but that the germs had, and he was living proof. Or not living maybe, but still proof, he corrected himself."

You can just see this kid's shit-eating grin, his wry self-correction. Hear that teenager's desire to charm, which, against the backdrop of his recent suffering, becomes all the more poignant:

The bad guys used to be Pakistan, and then they were Argentina and Turkey, and after that he had lost track. "What do you want me to tell you?" he asked, shrugging his shoulders. "Mostly I just miss my girlfriend." Her name was Tracey Tipton, and she did this thing with his earlobes and the notched edge of her front teeth that made his entire body go taut and buzz like a guitar string.

In that tiny capsule, I think you can really see the Kansas:Oz ratio: you've got Park Falls, Wisconsin; you've got some sort of murky, apocalyptic plague that has driven these souls into the City; and you also have Jeremy's shrug, his mock-casual affect and sincere confession of longing. These details strike me as exactly the way a sixteen-year-old boy from Park Falls, Wisconsin, *would* react to finding himself in an afterlife. Why should things make more sense in the afterlife, why should any of our questions get answered there? How can we even approach, in language, a loss so violent and extreme as the loss of *everything*? Against the scale of a global apocalypse, everything he misses, everything he's lost, condenses to this tiniest of gestures of his girlfriend's: a nibble on his earlobe. It's a heartbreaking, human detail, and one that makes me immediately willing to believe in the plague and this city of the dead.

Another example in which concrete and figurative details combine to nail down a fictional world occurs in Kelly Link's story "The Specialist's Hat," in which Link stages a tale about childhood grief in a possibly haunted mansion called Eight Chimneys:

Eight Chimneys has exactly one hundred windows, all still with the original wavery panes of handblown glass. With so many windows, Samantha thinks, Eight Chimneys should always be full of light, but instead the trees press close against the house, so that the rooms on the first and second story—even the third-story rooms—are green and dim, as if Samantha and Claire are living underneath the sea. This is the light that makes the tourists into ghosts.

These two sisters, Samantha and Claire, have recently lost their mother. In the description above, Link skillfully blends concrete details about the house itself, such as the number of windows and the "handblown" glass, with the girls' subjective experience of these "green and dim" rooms. We get a powerful sense of their isolation and their grief. During the day, we learn, Eight Chimneys is a tourist attraction: "The house is open to the public, and . . . people—families—driving along the Blue Ridge Parkway will stop to tour the grounds." But these cheerful visitors from the "real" world, far from making the rooms of Eight Chimneys any less mysterious, enhance our sense of the kids' seclusion. They really are just tourists, mere interlopers through the ghostly fog of the twins' grief. Our feeling for the girls' bereavement and isolation and the claustrophobia of Eight Chimneys (and of the private world of childhood more generally) is enhanced, not diminished, by Link's deft mention of the Blue Ridge Parkway. While family sedans go whizzing past on the highway, here is a stagnant pocket, a twilight zone. "The light that makes the tourists into ghosts" makes the sisters' grief palpable—it's a literal detail about the actual light in Eight

Chimneys, as well as a powerful evocation of these two characters' haunted interiors.

So, to add my two cents to O'Connor's original advice for "the person writing a fantasy": strict attention must be paid to your characters' inner lives. It's the characters' responses to their environment that will ultimately make their setting real for your readers. No matter how foreign or strange your imaginary world may initially appear, if your characters move through it in ways that feel "realistic"—if your characters' speech and behavior and moods and terrors ring true to what we know about their personalities and basic human nature—then your readers are far more likely to accept the place on its own terms. Through each character's reactions to his or her setting, important boundaries are erected—what's normal and what's abnormal in this alternate zone? Possible or impossible? Cheering or heartbreaking? Where does the danger reside? What is there to fear in a Narnia or a Macondo? This is how consequence gets established. "Raise the stakes," young writers frequently hear in workshops; in the case of an altered universe, I think this advice is particularly important. What do readers want? A world with pleasures and dangers that mirror our own, "so real that it is fantastic." Characters with something to gain or lose. Permission to care.

V. Hit the Ground Running

WHEN DOING SOMETHING weird, you can trust your reader to make adjustments if you hit the ground running. Let's examine three beginnings that launch our voyages into impossible realms.

They frontload the strangeness, and present it in O'Connor's "naturalistic vein" without elaborate explanation or apology. "Dorothy, you're not in Kansas anymore," these openings inform us.

1. When Gregor Samsa awoke one morning from troubled dreams, he found himself changed into a monstrous cockroach in his bed.

I love the unapologetic strangeness of this first line. A friend of mine calls this "the fish-slap-to-the-face technique"—there is no effort made to gradually acclimate the reader, no accommodation for our disbelief. We are thrown into Gregor Samsa's altered reality at the precise moment that he is tap-tapping his insect body for the first time. Practically, this is a wonderful strategy, in terms of exposition and pacing—we learn the ropes with him.

2. When the blind man arrived in the city, he claimed that he had traveled across a desert of living sand. First he had died, he said, and then—snap—the desert. He told the story to everyone who would listen, bobbing his head to follow the sound of their footsteps. Showers of red grit fell from his beard.

Here is another great example of a balanced ratio of Oz mystique and Kansas mortar, courtesy of Kevin Brockmeier. This chatty blind man claims to be both newly dead and newly arrived from a desert of "living sand"—who is this nut job? Imagine if somebody walked into a Starbucks and told you that! But when his head bobs, "showers of red grit" fall out of his beard. A fine shower of support for the blind man's story. Really, though, that "snap" is what does it for me. His hunger to be listened to by anybody, everybody—his bobbing insistence—these gestures and attitudes feel so recognizable, so human, that they confirm the blind man for me as a real person, someone so attentively, lovingly observed by Brockmeier that he becomes a character with a soul, whose testimony I can trust.

3. *The causes of the rapid extinction of the Dinosaur remain mysterious; the species had evolved and grown throughout the Triassic and the Jurassic, and for 150 million years the Dinosaur had been the undisputed master of the continents. Perhaps the species was unable to adapt to the great changes of climate and vegetation which took place in the Cretaceous period. By its end all the Dinosaurs were dead.*

All except me,—Qfwfq corrected,—because, for a certain period, I was also a Dinosaur: about fifty million years, I'd say, and I don't regret it; if you were a Dinosaur in those days, you were sure you were in the right, and you made everyone look up to you.

This is the opening from my favorite Italo Calvino story, "The Dinosaurs." Here we get a spectacular leap from Kansas into Oz— we start with a dry epigraph that could be from a science textbook, and then, whiplash fast, we are listening to the gregarious first-person rant of Qfwfq (whom I've always pictured as the dinosaur version of a boozy Italian uncle). The matter-of-fact, chatty tone suggests that we readers can relax and let go of the ordinary questions that might occur to one when confronted with such an out-landish premise ("How did this ancient reptile survive?," "How did he learn English?," "Was Stephen Jay Gould right about the end of the Cretaceous?," et cetera.) The authority of Qfwfq's first-person voice, his storyteller's charisma, gives us permission to go on reading with a similarly relaxed and joyful attitude. Right away, Calvino makes it clear that he's set his story so far outside the realm of possibility that there's no need to be troubled by logistic questions about the premise, or the setting, or just how, exactly, a prehistoric refugee like Qfwfq could be stowed away in our century.

One final note, since I've talked so much about the importance of concrete detail to engineers of fantasy worlds. O'Connor also warns against the "accretion of mere detail": overdescription, data accumulation. You want to anticipate the kinds of questions that are going to occur to your reader, but it's good to remember that readers don't necessarily need or even particularly want answers to all the questions that occur to them. There might be a way inside the text to acknowledge the questions. Perhaps your character is equally baffled, which happens in *The Metamorphosis*; Gregor doesn't know why he is a cockroach. Omission is also an art. In one of the most beautifully mysterious moments in *The Brief History of the Dead*, a young woman, Graciela Cavazos, is asked how she came to the city. Brockmeier writes, "Graciela Cavazos would say only that she began to snow—four words—and smile bashfully whenever anyone pressed her for details."

VI. The Purpose

THE BELIEVER PUBLISHED an interview between Ben Marcus and George Saunders from which I shamelessly recite whenever students anxiously ask me if they are permitted to write "weird" fiction. Marcus asks:

I'm interested in the trace fantastical elements that appear in your stories, as well as the occasional ghost. So much of your stories seem wedded to an emotional realism, yet your settings—the landscapes—are often, if not fantastical, then exceedingly odd or improbable, leading to real emotions in an unreal world. And then your stories, sometimes very slightly, leave the realm of physical possibility entirely (the dead awaken, for instance). Are these three distinct-writing spaces to you? Do you see a difference between "realism" and fantastical writing?

To which Saunders replies: "Realism is nonsense when you think of it. I mean, there is no such thing. Nobody writes realism, if realism is defined as 'fiction that is objective and real and not distorted, but is just, you know, normal.' . . . The nature of all fiction is distortion, exaggeration, and compression . . . What I find exciting is the idea that no work of fiction will ever, ever, come close to 'documenting' life. So then, the purpose of it must be otherwise."

What *is* the purpose, then?

Why spend so much energy to create an imaginary place?

I speak as a person who has several male relations who refuse on principle to read fiction at all, fantastic or realistic. Their rationale goes something like this: "What truth can I learn from some whoppers told by a damn elf, or an asshole on a road trip, or a make-believe Russian in outer space?" Historical fiction occasionally gets a grudging pass, because at least it teaches one about period dress and "customs." But Oz, Eight Chimneys, the City of the Dead—get out of here! What's the value in spending a chunk of your life in a place that doesn't exist?

And here comes Flannery O'Connor again, preaching to our choir: "The truth is not distorted here," she writes, "but rather a distortion is used to get at truth." We exit these Oz places with a renewed sense of wonder, and with an altered understanding of our own lives and bodies and boundaries; with a looser relationship, too, perhaps, to that undulating set of memories and perceptions and sensations, the engulfing sum, of "everyday reality." As Shirley Jackson, another engineer of impossible architectures, writes as she opens a door onto infinite corridors in "The Haunting of Hill House": "No live organism can continue for long to exist sanely under conditions of absolute reality; even larks and katydids are supposed, by some, to dream."

ENDINGS:
Parting Is Such Sweet Sorrow

ELISSA SCHAPPELL

"GREAT IS THE art of beginning," Longfellow said, "but greater the art of ending."

It's true. Beginnings, like first kisses, need only seduce us with their potential, clearly establish the theme, cast, and tenor of the affair to come, whereas the ending must realize the story's potential, deliver on the checks the beginning has signed, and do so in such a memorable way that the reader is left wanting more. For we may forget how a relationship began—we were drunk, it was wartime, it began slowly—but rarely do we forget how it ended—with a slap, a kiss tasting of tears, a farewell wave from the back of a camel. It's the end of the story we're focused on when we recount these tales of betrayal, lost love, infidelity, isn't it?

The ending bears all the weight of the story, its task nothing less than imbuing the story with meaning and making it unforgettable. The ending must fulfill the reader's expectations by answering the questions that have been raised in the reader's mind (or at least some of them), and it has to make sense, but at the same time, it should be unexpected. I don't mean I want a surprise—I mean, even if I know how the story will end, I want to be surprised by the way I get there. The writer has done his job, novelist David Leavitt says, when the reader's reaction to the ending is "Oh my God," followed by "Of course."

Obviously, endings are hard. Every writer struggles with them. Ernest Hemingway revised the last page of *A Farewell to Arms* thirty-nine times. When asked in an interview what the problem was that had him in such a swivet, he answered, "Getting the words right."

Oh, is that all?

If beginnings are characterized by a lot of throat clearing and exposition, and the middle is where the writer hits his stride, endings—the knowledge that the end is near, *The C on my A-B-C narrative arc looms!*—strikes panic in writers' hearts. You have to understand your story to end your story. Endings are harder than beginnings because they must grow organically out of the rest. They must, as Anton Chekhov says, "artfully concentrate for the reader an impression of the entire work."

Of course, certain genres require specific closures. Mysteries, crime novels, ghost stories, bodice rippers, all by their very nature promise a neat resolution. Once the reader knows "who done it" and how; what, pray tell, ate those Eagle Scouts; and who will end up in whose arms, there is no reason for the author to stick around. Indeed, it's best just to tidy up quickly and get out of there as elegantly as possible. Part of the pleasure of reading these genres is knowing exactly what sort of ending we can expect, and that our desires will be satisfied. But in fiction writing, it is often less clear to the writer how an ending should be resolved. Here are some common approaches—both ones to aspire to and ones to avoid—when writing an ending.

The Doogie Howser Ending

THE PRESSURE TO tell readers what we want them to know is strong. Oftentimes, this anxiety manifests itself in the last paragraph of the piece being written in the form of summation, telling our readers what we fear we haven't shown them, or what Rob Spillman, the editor of *Tin House* magazine, calls a "Doogie Howser at the typewriter" moment. *Doogie Howser, M.D.* was a television show in the early nineties starring Neil Patrick Harris as a relentlessly perky teen doctor. At the close of every episode, Doogie would sit down at the typewriter and bang out the take-away ("Today I learned that friends are invaluable"), just in case you missed it.

The cure for Howsering is simple: amputate the offending paragraph or paragraphs and be done with it. I realize that sounds heartless and cruel, but buck up, darling. You're in grand company. William Faulkner was speaking from experience when he advised writers to "murder your darlings." Understand that most early drafts are greatly improved by tearing off the first and last pages. If excising the last paragraph or page doesn't reveal an ending that feels true, then go back. Retrace your steps and return to the place where you last felt a pulse, where the language felt alive, and you felt engaged. If that's not your ending, it will at least point you true north.

The Overly Symbolic Ending

IT ISN'T UNCOMMON for an author, anxious about his woefully unsatisfying ending, to attempt to seduce readers by getting them drunk on poetics, overripe similes and metaphors, and the low-hanging fruit of symbolism, in the hopes that some über-image will emerge to which the reader can attach profound meaning. That said, ending with a resonant image, one that hearkens back to the beginning or middle of the story, can be an effective way to illuminate your story's theme.

Amy Hempel's "In the Cemetery Where Al Jolson Is Buried" opens with the narrator in a hospital visiting her best friend, who is dying of a terminal illness. Despite intimations that the best friend has been sick for a while, this is the first time the narrator has been able to force herself to come. The only way she can cope is by cracking jokes and sharing trivia. One anecdote the nameless narrator shares is about the first chimpanzee to learn sign language. "'Did you know that when they taught the first chimp to talk, it lied?'" she says. The best friend laughs gamely; however, when the narrator asks if she wants to hear the rest of the story, warning her, "'it will break your heart,'" the friend demurs.

At story's end, after the best friend has died, the narrator, filled with grief, claims she can remember nothing about this time, only the trivial details. She closes:

In the course of the experiment, that chimp had a baby. Imagine how her trainers must have thrilled when the mother, without prompting, began to sign to her newborn. Baby, drink milk. Baby, play ball.

And when the baby died, the mother stood over the body, her wrinkled hands moving with animal grace, forming again and again the words, Baby, come hug, Baby, come hug, fluent now in the language of grief.

This bit of trivia brings the story full circle. The reader couldn't have predicted that the chimp, referenced only twice earlier, would be the image Hempel would use to finish the story; but by ending with the bereft chimp unable to process such an overwhelming loss, Hempel communicates the depth of the narrator's grief, the universal grief we all experience, without sentimentality, leaving the reader positively devastated.

So go for it. Just remember that should you choose to end your story with a killer image, one you hope will pull the story together and resonate for the reader, be subtle. Be wary of being heavy-handed and always be on guard for the cliché—the train leaving the station, the reunited lovers riding off into the distance, the character gazing at the sunset/ sunrise/moon. Of course, there are exceptions. In one of the greatest endings in all of literature, F. Scott Fitzgerald's *The Great Gatsby* famously leaves Nick Carraway contemplating Gatsby looking out at the green light at the end of Daisy's dock across the Long Island Sound, the last line serving as a coda: "So we beat on, boats against the current, borne back ceaselessly into the past."

In that moment, the story expands, and we can imagine the whole world breathing.

The Epilogue Ending

IN THE WAY that a coda, intended to elegantly enhance the theme of the story, can in the wrong hands hit the reader like a cudgel, so it is with epilogues. While I do not shudder the way I do when I see that a novel has a prologue, the sight of an epilogue always fills me with skepticism. Epilogues must be more than a double ending, or a hint at a sequel. If you feel compelled to pen an epilogue, make sure that it springs organically from the text, that it enhances your theme, and that it adds a new dimension to the story.

The inclusion of an epilogue permitted Margaret Atwood to provide two endings to her feminist dystopian satire *The Hand-maid's Tale*. The plot of the novel, set in a not-so-distant future America where white racist religious fanatics exert complete control over the lives and reproductive rights of women, ends on an ambiguous note, the reader unsure of the fate of the heroine, Offred. However, the epilogue, presented in the form of notes from an academic symposium in the future, suggests that Offred escaped and the world she inhabited is history. The last line of the epilogue, "Are there any questions?" has such power, some of the book's fans have had it tattooed on their bodies.

The Epiphanic Ending

EPIPHANIES ARE WILDLY popular and understandably so, as an epiphany can provide the author with a way to crystallize his or her themes and finish on a ringing emotional high note. The author hopes that as the world comes into hyperfocus for a character in the throes of an epiphany it will also for the reader. However, an epiphany in and of itself doesn't constitute an ending. If an epiphany is unearned, illogical, or ends the story too soon, the writer has failed. Most often, the action that follows this moment of acute awareness is the true end of a story. When you find yourself aching to strike your character down with an epiphany, a blazing comet of clarity that changes everything, make sure it can be followed by an action that warrants being your ending. Despite the fact that James Joyce's characters, particularly those Dubliners, experience epiphanies as though they were seasonal allergies, in reality epiphanies are rare, and often fleeting. As they should be. Joyce's short masterpiece "The Dead" begins, appropriately enough, at a celebration of the religious holiday the Feast of the Epiphany. During the party, a tenor sings for the guests, as the protagonist, Gabriel, observes a woman—who, after a moment, he realizes is his wife, Gretta— transfixed by the song. Later, in their hotel, a wistful Gretta confesses that the song stirred memories of an old love who despite suffering from consumption had stood vigil outside her window in a storm the night before she left Galway for Dublin and subsequently died. The story closes with Gabriel realizing that he has never and will never love his wife as this man did. Joyce writes: "His soul swooned slowly as he heard the snow falling faintly through the universe and faintly falling, like the descent of their last end, upon all the living and the dead."

The No-End-in-Sight Ending

IT IS NOT difficult to get lost inside your story and to become unsure of the direction in which your denouement lies, or, recognizing this, to fail to stop and reorient yourself, but rather charge on ahead, believing that if you keep plunging forward through the thickets of confusion, you will, by magic, happy accident, or providence, reach the nirvana of a perfect ending. The reality is that at some juncture—half blind, fingers cramped into gnarled fists, family and friends banging on your door—you will be forced to acknowledge that you are overwriting.

But before you allow yourself to be sucked down into the quicksand of despair, pause; it is easy—in theory, at least—to save yourself. All that are required are a machete, a wheelbarrow, a handkerchief, and nerve.

Consider that there may simply be too much going on for any mortal to bring the story to a close in a sane and satisfactory fashion. The only way to see the end is to clear all the narrative brush, mercilessly hack away at the overgrowth of nonessential scenes, dialogue, and action. Sever competing story lines, cart them away in your wheelbarrow. Turn a cold eye on your cast. Is it too large? Are all of the characters contributing? Every character comes with drama; if some are receiving more attention than their parts warrant, bid them a fond adieu. If you can't bear the thought of cutting them loose altogether, transfer them into the reserves file. Take your handkerchief, mop your brow, and now look at your story. The path to your ending should be much clearer.

The Open Ending

THE FLIP SIDE of the story that goes on without end is, of course, the story that just stops, like a conversation in which the speaker is cut off midsentence. You find this often in the work of writers who are attempting to mimic literary masters such as Virginia Woolf, Ernest Hemingway, and especially Anton Chekhov, who is credited with popularizing what is known as the "open" or "zero" ending.

The open ending doesn't focus on building the story to a resolution of conflict (or at least not the one we expected) or an epiphany. Rarely do we see how a character has changed, but rather, more realistically, how the character has failed to change; or if there's been change, it's dubious. Because of this, open-ended stories possess a true-to-life, naturalistic quality. By subverting our expectations, the author forces us to project our own meaning onto the end. So the epiphany isn't in the character; instead, that moment of illumination occurs within the reader, which can be much more powerful than the experience we'd have witnessing a character's epiphany on the page.

Many of John Cheever's stories and the majority of Raymond Carver's end with a character arrested in thought or on the verge of a realization, as Nick is at the end of Carver's "What We Talk About When We Talk About Love." The gin is drunk up, the kitchen has grown dark, and the two couples, having grown increasingly inarticulate and frustrated by their attempts to define the elusive nature of love, sit in silence. Carver expresses the universal desire for love by having Nick reflect on the "the human noise we sat there making"—the beating of their hearts.

The key to creating a successful open ending is to leave the reader with a powerful impression of what the future might hold for a character, a sense of how his or her view of the world has been altered in a significant way. Despite the fact that the story is drawing to a close, you want the reader to feel the story has, in the end, gotten bigger, not smaller.

Or, as a character says in Grace Paley's short story "A Conversation with My Father," by way of explaining to her father why she doesn't write traditional stories: "Everyone, real or invented, deserves the open destiny of life."

Open. Not empty. Understand that should you end your story too soon, or too abruptly, your readers will most likely not interpret your silence and sudden exit for depth or mystery or artful obscurity. They will think you walked away to have a cigarette.

And oh that knowing your last line guaranteed you a stellar ending. If you are lucky, you might find—as Charles D'Ambrosio did when he decided to begin his moving story "Drummond & Son" with the challenge to write a story that ends with a father saying, "I love you" to his troubled son—that the last line can be the seed that grows the story. However, the risk in having a predetermined final line is that the story can feel overdetermined, the connections forced and artificial. Knowing where you're going is swell, just make sure that you leave yourself open to discovery in the writing. When there's no discovery in the writer, there's no discovery in the reader.

The Big Bang Ending

FOR AN AUTHOR to feel trapped in a story, claustrophobic, bored, frustrated, perhaps even angry, is not unheard of. Desperate to bring this sorry situation to a dramatic conclusive end, he or she unleashes an earthquake, a flood, a fire, a plague of frogs; strangles grandma in front of her dachshunds; sinks a ship filled with refugee children; throws the smirking pedophile into a cage of tigers, hoping that this extreme or tragic ending will do the emotional work the author could not. When in fact, such bald and cheap attempts to provoke readers, to make them angry, or to bring them to tears will inspire only disappointment and ultimately leave them feeling empty.

Gratuitous endings are unforgivable. However, extreme endings that are earned, that are consistent with the story line and what we know of the characters, can make for a brutally successful ending.

Flannery O'Connor, patron saint of peafowl and the Southern grotesque form, is famous for unsettling, tragicomic endings punctuated by bursts of violence. We look forward to these dependably grim and deliciously ironic endings, the attendant losses of life and salvation, because O'Connor creates characters who, deeply flawed in the eyes of God, and thus in her eyes as well, get what they deserve. It is a testament to O'Connor's gift for dark comedy and storytelling that we allow ourselves to be implicated in the final judgment she passes on her characters. We are amused by the twist on fate O'Connor delivers at the end of "Good Country People," when the haughty young woman's attempted seduction of a simple country Bible salesman ends with him stealing her artificial leg, and horrified at the close of "A Good Man Is Hard to Find," which famously ends with the self-serving, irritating grandmother being executed. As though we didn't already feel guilty for wishing somebody would shut grandma up, O'Connor's choice to end the story with dialogue— "'She would of been a good woman,' The Misfit said, 'if it had been somebody there to shoot her every minute of her life'"— removes the buffer between reader and author, putting us on the scene so we can almost smell the sulfur. Which is why this ending lodges itself in the reader's memory like a bullet.

The Happy Ending

EVERYBODY LIKES A happy ending, readers *and* writers. So ingrained is this belief in the author's mind that if he reunites the lovers, graces the infertile couple with not one, but two children, saves the earth from being pulled into the sun, he will win the reader's heart. But you must, as with all endings, earn your happiness. If the reader doesn't have good reason to imagine the story *won't* end happily, then the happy ending is worthless. We suspect that Charles Dickens's stouthearted orphan David Copperfield will indeed become the hero of his own life but that his journey will be fraught. And it is. David endures all manner of loss and tribulation, but the greatest tragedy is his having married Dora, of whom he is very fond, but does not love, while pining for Agnes. In order for David to marry Agnes, Dickens must off Dora. So while David gets his happy ending, it comes at a cost.

The Sad Ending

AND IT IS just as important, if not more so, for an author to earn a sad ending, because the truth is readers are more likely to overlook a slightly flimsy happy ending (after all, they've got the sun on their shoulders) than a poorly developed sad one (after all, it's midnight in their soul and they're standing in a downpour). As with the happy ending, if readers don't have reason to believe that there's the smallest chance the story will end, if not happily, then not miserably—the sad ending will not be nearly as satisfying.

Don't think for a moment that by simply offing the beloved heroine or by drowning a sack of kittens, you will break your reader's heart. You have to earn your tears. No tears in the writer, no tears in the reader. I believe it must have pained Edith Wharton awfully to have the splendid Lily Bart die at the end of *The House of Mirth*, just at the moment of redemption: "He knelt by the bed and bent over her, draining their last moment to its lees; and in the silence there passed between them the word which made all clear."

And despite the classification of an ending being either "happy" or "sad," the finales that linger in the reader's mind are those that are tinged with a little of both.

The Moralistic Ending

THERE IS NEVER any doubt how a fable or fairy tale is going to end—with a moral. Only the most unsophisticated fiction, that geared toward preaching/educating/controlling the behavior of children (and dim-witted children, at that), ends with the reader being taught a lesson. I don't know about you, but I don't care to be lectured to, not by an elephant or a goblin or a wise man in a robe clutching a staff. It's tedious. If you want to end on a moral note, make sure you do so obliquely. I shouldn't be aware that I've drunk the Kool-Aid until I'm in line to join the merchant marines.

The Symmetrical Ending

I KNOW NO one likes to admit it, but at some point every author feels the temptation to pen a terribly clever ending. Here I should say that I applaud cleverness and experimentation, but never for the pure sake of being clever or experimental. Should you want to experiment with an ingenious ending, one effective means is to create a symmetry between your beginning and your ending, as Hemingway does in *For Whom the Bell Tolls*, which opens and closes with Robert Jordan awaiting the firing squad on the pine-needled floor of a forest, or as Marcel Proust does in *In Search of Lost Time*, which begins and ends with a reference to time.

If you grew up, as I did, in the 1970s, you might have had your mind blown, as I did, when you discovered that S. E. Hinton's classic American coming-of-age novel *The Outsiders* (written when she was just sixteen) begins and ends with the same line: "When I stepped out into the bright sunlight, from the darkness of the movie house, I had only two things on my mind: Paul Newman, and a ride home." The novel opens with Ponyboy Curtis, a member of the hardscrabble Greasers gang, being jumped by members of a rival gang—the middle-class Socs—as he leaves a movie theater. It closes with Ponyboy, who has barely survived the turf war that took the lives of his brother and friends, beginning a writing assignment for his English class, suggesting that the story we just read was Ponyboy's account of the events. Of course, there are other, more sophisticated modern pieces with beginnings and endings that mirror each other. For example, Lydia Davis's microportrait of a marriage "In a House Besieged," employs the title as both the first and last lines, the cadence of the lines creating an inescapable continuum mimicking the couple's relationship.

The *Surprise!* Ending

SURPRISE ENDINGS ARE seductive because they appear to offer the promise of an easy end to our problems. The oldest surprise ending in the book, the deus ex machina, comes from Horace's *Ars Poetica*, in which he cautions poets never to resort to creating a "god from the machine" to resolve their conflicts. Horace was reacting to Euripides's fondness for concluding a play by introducing a new character, most often a god, who, suspended from a crane by a leather harness, would be lowered on to the stage to save the day for no reason that made sense. (Witness Medea, guilty of murder and infanticide, being whisked off to Athens before Jason can exact his revenge.)

For those of you taking notes, this means no happy coincidence, no emergence of a character or man in a leather harness who will save the day. No *And then I woke up!* There is a tale, now legendary in the circles of teachers of creative writing, about a story that ends with the revelation that the story was being narrated by a squirrel with a bag on its head, which is the explanation for the story's problem with point of view.

However, if you're set on writing a surprise ending, a real shocker, it must be original—in a good way, not a narrated-by-vermin way—which is hard in this day and age, when we seem almost unshockable.

Perhaps the most famous surprise ending in modern literature is from Ambrose Bierce's 1890 classic short story "An Occurrence at Owl Creek Bridge," which opens with Peyton Farquhar standing on a bridge with a noose around his neck, about to be hanged for being a Confederate sympathizer. What follows appears to be the tale of his desperate escape—he makes his way home to his wife. But, in fact, the last third of the story is imagined in the span of time between his falling from the bridge and the noose snapping his neck: "As he is about to clasp her he feels a stunning blow on the back of the neck; a blinding white light blazes all about him with a sound like the shock of a cannon—then all is darkness and silence!"

A lot of amateur writers seem to favor the surprise ending of "An Occurrence at Owl Creek Bridge," perhaps because it's a story that's often taught to high school students, an age at which too many writers leave off reading. However, it is a respectable trope, albeit one that can leave audiences howling in furious bewilderment. Witness the last episode of *The Sopranos* (a tragedy worthy of Shakespeare), which could be interpreted as showing that six seasons worth of story were all a flashback of the main character, who is about to be capped.

The Make-the-Reader-Wait-for-It Ending

IF YOU HAVE done your job well, readers' anticipation of your ending has been building. Their natural reaction is one of excitement, the heart rate increases and so does the speed at which they read. All they want to do is gallop toward the finish line, thoughtlessly skimming over sentences you've labored over. Stop them. Pull on the reins! Never do you want to let your readers out of your control, least of all at the end. You want them fully attuned to every word, every nuance. One of the most effective ways to accomplish this is by engaging the reader on as many sensory levels as possible, so as to ground them entirely in the moment.

The ending of Kate Chopin's *The Awakening* is exquisite torture. Chopin doles out the sensory details as she puts the reader in the body of Edna, a wife and mother filled with the knowledge that she will never be able to live her life truly as she pleases, standing on the beach:

> The water of the Gulf stretched out before her, gleaming with the million lights of the sun. The voice of the sea is seductive,

never ceasing, whispering, clamoring, murmuring, inviting the soul to wander in abysses of solitude. All along the white beach, up and down, there was no living thing in sight. A bird with a broken wing was beating the air above, reeling, fluttering, circling disabled down, down to the water.

We experience the sensation of cold as Edna wades naked into the water, the exhaustion of her body as she swims away from shore, and ultimately her final thoughts as she drowns:

> Edna heard her father's voice and her sister Margaret's. She heard the barking of an old dog that was chained to the sycamore tree. The spurs of the cavalry officer clanged as he walked across the porch. There was the hum of bees, and the musky odor of pinks filled the air.

Chopin's vivid details and lyrical prose draw us so deeply into the character of Edna, we can almost taste the salt on our lips.

Every word, every sentence in a story or novel should count. However, never is it more crucial, never does the language bear more weight than in the final line. The last line should be the perfect crystallization of the story. If you write a sublime last line that resonates with readers, they will hold it fast, repeat it like poetry, until it takes on the weight of prayer.

Sometimes these lines are like a pop on the jaw, as with Hemingway's *The Sun Also Rises*, which closes with his alter ego, Jake, responding to Brett's notion they could have be happy together: "'Yes,' I said. 'Isn't it pretty to think so?'"—a gimlet-eyed distillation of Jake's, and the author's, resignation. Sure, we all have hopes and dreams, but they are just that. Or the line can land like a punch in the gut. In *1984*, George Orwell holds out the hope that Winston will escape the totalitarian regime and overthrow the government until the last line: "He loved Big Brother." The message Orwell delivers is loud and unmistakable: those who succumb are done.

Then there are those who go long, as Salman Rushdie does, expertly controlling the reader through the footfall-like rhythms of his words as they build to a run at the close of *Midnight's Children*:

> Yes, they will trample me underfoot, the numbers marching one two three, four hundred million five hundred six, reducing me to specks of voiceless dust, just as, all in good time, they will trample my son who is not my son, and his son who will not be his, and his who will not be his, until the thousand and first generation, until a thousand and one midnights have bestowed their terrible gifts and a thousand and one children have died, because it is the privilege and the curse of midnight's children to be both masters and victims of their times, to forsake privacy and be sucked into the annihilating whirlpool of the multitudes, and to be unable to live or die in peace.

In Conclusion

IT ALL COMES down to this: endings are a bitch. The best ending is one that leaves readers with a profound sense of awe and wonder, not only at the world the author has created but also at the considerable skill with which the writer has pulled it off. The truth is, the best endings don't feel like endings at all. The best ending is one in which the world gets larger, not smaller. It's not an ending at all. It's the beginning of understanding the world and ourselves in a new way.

CONTRIBUTORS

STEVE ALMOND is the author, most recently, of the story collection *God Bless America*.

ANDREA BARRETT is the author of six novels, most recently *The Air We Breathe*, and two collections of short fiction, *Ship Fever*, which received the National Book Award, and *Servants of the Map*, a finalist for the Pulitzer Prize. She's been a MacArthur fellow and a fellow at the Center for Scholars and Writers at the New York Public Library and has also received Guggenheim and NEA fellowships. She lives in western Massachusetts and teaches at Williams College.

CHRISTOPHER R. BEHA is the author of a memoir, *The Whole Five Feet*, and a novel, *What Happened to Sophie Wilder*. He contributes regularly to the *New York Times Book Review*, the *London Review of Books*, and *Harper's*, where he works as an associate editor.

AIMEE BENDER is the author of four books; the most recent, *The Particular Sadness of Lemon Cake*, won a SCIBA Award and an Alex Award, and has been translated into sixteen languages. Her short fiction has been published in *Tin House*, *Granta*, the *Paris Review*, *McSweeney's*, *Harper's*, as well as heard on *This American Life* and *Selected Shorts*. She has been a regular faculty member at the Tin House Summer Writer's Conference and teaches during the school year at USC.

ADAM BRAVER is the author of *Misfit; November 22, 1963; Mr. Lincoln's Wars; Divine Sarah;* and *Crows Over the Wheatfield*. His work has appeared in journals such as *Harvard Review, Tin House, Dœdalus, Ontario Review*, the *Normal School*, and *West Branch*. He is writer-in-residence at Roger Williams University.

ANTHONY DOERR lives in Boise, Idaho. He's the author of four books, *The Shell Collector, About Grace, Four Seasons in Rome*, and, most recently, *Memory Wall*. His short fiction has won four O. Henry Prizes and has been anthologized in *The Best American Short Stories, The Anchor Book of New American Short Stories*, and *The Scribner Anthology of Contemporary Fiction*. Among the prizes his work has won are the Barnes & Noble Discover Prize, the Rome Prize, the New York Public Library's Young Lions Fiction Award, a Guggenheim Fellowship, the National Magazine Award for Fiction, the Story Prize, and the 2011 London Sunday Times EFG Short Story Award.

ANN HOOD is the author of thirteen books, including the bestselling novels *The Knitting Circle* and *The Red Thread* and the memoir *Comfort: A Journey through Grief*, which was a New York Times Editors Choice and chosen as one of the top ten nonfiction books of 2008 by *Entertainment Weekly*. A regular contributor to the *New York Times* and NPR's *The Story* with Dick Gordon, she has won two Pushcart Prizes, and Best American Spiritual Writing, Travel Writing, and Food Writing awards.

BRET ANTHONY JOHNSTON is the author of *Corpus Christi: Stories* and the editor of *Naming the World and Other Exercises for the Creative Writer*. His work has recently appeared in the *Atlantic Monthly, Esquire, The Best American Short Stories 2011,* and *The Pushcart Prize 2012.* He is the director of creative writing at Harvard University and can be reached at www. bretanthonyjohnston.com.

JIM KRUSOE is the author of the novels *Parsifal, Toward You, Erased, Girl Factory,* and *Iceland;* two collections of stories; and five books of poetry. He is the recipient of fellowships from the National Endowment for the Arts and the Lila Wallace Reader's Digest Fund. He teaches at Santa Monica College and lives in Los Angeles.

ANTONYA NELSON is the author of four novels, including *Bound* (Bloomsbury, 2010) and six short story collections, including *Nothing Right* (Bloomsbury, 2009). Her work has appeared in the *New Yorker, Esquire, Harper's, Redbook,* and many other magazines, as well as in anthologies such as *Prize Stories: The O. Henry Awards* and *The Best American Short Stories.* She is the recipient of a USA Artists Award in 2009, the 2003 Rea Award for Short Fiction, as well as NEA and Guggenheim fellowships, and teaches in the Warren Wilson College

MFA Program, as well as in the University of Houston's Creative Writing Program. She lives in Telluride, Colorado; Las Cruces, New Mexico; and Houston, Texas.

MAGGIE NELSON is the author of four books of nonfiction and four books of poetry, including *The Art of Cruelty: A Reckoning* (Norton, 2011), *Bluets* (Wave Books, 2009), *Women, the New York School, and Other True Abstractions* (University of Iowa, 2007), *The Red Parts: A Memoir* (Free Press, 2007), and *Jane: A Murder* (Soft Skull, 2005). She has been awarded a Guggenheim in Nonfiction, an NEA in Poetry, and a Creative Capital/Andy Warhol Foundation grant for Art Writing. Currently she teaches at CalArts in Valencia, California, and lives in Los Angeles.

BENJAMIN PERCY is the author of two novels, *Red Moon* (forthcoming from Grand Central/Hachette in 2013) and *The Wilding*, as well as two books of short stories, *Refresh, Refresh* and *The Language of Elk*. His fiction and nonfiction have been read on National Public Radio and published by *Esquire*, *GQ*, *Time*, *Men's Journal*, *Outside*, the *Wall Street Journal*, and the *Paris Review*. His honors include a Whiting Writers Award, a grant from the National Endowment for the Arts, a Pushcart Prize, a Plimpton Prize, and inclusion in *The Best American Short Stories* and *The Best American Comics*.

KAREN RUSSELL is the author of the 2007 story collection *St. Lucy's Home for Girls Raised by Wolves* and the 2011 novel *Swamplandia!* Her stories have been published in the *New Yorker*, *Granta*, and *The Best American Short Sto-*

ries anthology, and her second story collection, *Vampires in the Lemon Grove*, will be published by Alfred A. Knopf in 2013.

ELISSA SCHAPPELL is the author of two books of fiction, *Use Me* and, most recently, *Blueprints for Building Better Girls*, which was chosen by *O, The Oprah Magazine* as one of the Top 5 Books of 2011; by the *San Francisco Chronicle*, the *Boston Globe*, and the *Wall Street Journal* as a Best Book of 2011; and by *Newsweek/Daily Beast Writers* as one of the Favorite Books of 2011. She is co-editor with Jenny Offill of two anthologies, *The Friend Who Got Away* and *Money Changes Everything*. Her nonfiction has appeared in such places as *SPIN*, *Vogue*, *Real Simple*, *GQ*, the *Paris Review*, *Book Forum*, and the *New York Times Book Review*. Her fiction has appeared in journals such as *One Story*, *Nerve*, *BOMB*, and *The Literarian*. She is currently a contributing editor at *Vanity Fair*, and editor-at-large of *Tin House*. She teaches at NYU and in the low-residency MFA program at Queens University in Charlotte, North Carolina, and lives in Brooklyn.

MARY SZYBIST received her MFA from the Iowa Writers' Workshop. Her first collection of poems, *Granted*, was a finalist for the National Book Critics Circle Award, and her second collection, *Incarnadine*, is forthcoming from Graywolf Press in 2013. Szybist has received fellowships and awards from the National Endowment for the Arts, the Witter Bynner Foundation, the Library of Congress, the Rona Jaffe Foundation, the Great Lakes Colleges Association, and the Rockefeller Foundation's Bellagio Center. Her poems have appeared or are forthcoming in *Ploughshares*, *Virginia Quarterly Review*, *Poetry*, *Tin House*, the *Iowa Review,* the *Kenyon Review,* and other journals. She lives in Portland, Oregon, where she teaches at Lewis & Clark College.

COPYRIGHT NOTES AND PERMISSIONS